UNBREAKABLE

MASTERING YOUR MIND | BODY | LIFE

VICTOR IMHANS

Copyright © 2025 by Victor Imhans

Open House Books

ALL RIGHTS RESERVED

Except as permitted under the United States Copyright Act of 1976, no part of this book may be reproduced, distributed, or transmitted in any form or by any means or stored in a database or retrieval system without the prior written permission of the publisher, except in the case of brief quotations embodied in critical reviews and specific other noncommercial uses permitted by copyright law.

ISBN: 979-8-9922777-3-9 (Paperback)

TABLE OF CONTENTS

The Unbreakable Mindset Introduction 1
Section One: Improved Understanding 5
    Recognizing Your Mental Power 6
    Building Mental Resilience 9
    Overcoming Negative Thoughts 12
    Emotional and Mental Intelligence 18
    Navigating Emotions and Relationships 21
Section Two: Developing Your Body 27
    Diet for Ideal Health 33
    Rest and Recover: The Authority of Renewal 42
    Trauma Healing: Reclaiming Your Body 43
    The Road to an Unbreakable Life 48
Section Three: Learning About Your Life 49
    The Authority of Intention Living 50
    Your Road to Mastery of Your Life 56
    How to Create Harmony 59
Section Four: Dominating Your Environs 61
    The Effect of Your Surroundings 62
    Finding Work-Life Balance 67
    Financial Wellness 69
    The Authority of a Synced Environment 72
    Mirror of Your Values 73
Section Five: Developing Your Future 77
    Accepting Transformation 78
    Encouraging Creativity and Innovation 80

Constructing a Resilient and Reward Future 83

The Legacy and Creativity Play 86

Section Six: Resilience and Emotional Regulation Development............ 89

The Significance of Emotional Intelligence and Resilience.................... 90

Personal Development and Emotional Mastery 92

The Synergy of Emotional Mastery and Resilience 101

Making Your Dream a Reality... 102

Section Seven: Creating Future Worthful Relationships 105

Important Elements of Relationship Resilience..................................... 106

The Foundation of Connection: Active Listening................................. 107

Motivation in Social Interactions.. 108

Motivation and Resilience in Action 111

Section Eight: Shape a Future Anchored on Health 113

Why Put Health First in the Future?.. 114

The Ripple Impact of Giving Health Top Priority 117

The Role of Resilience in Medical Education.. 117

Techniques for Long-Term Wellness 121

Constructing a Sustainable Healthy Life.. 125

The health-First Perspective.. 129

Section Nine: Focusing on a Future-Based Career.................................. 135

Developing Professional Resilience 136

Maintaining Motivation for Professional Growth 137

Putting Your Career in the Future.. 139

Section Ten: Nurturing Creativity and Innovation................................. 141

Both ingenuity and perseverance are important aspects of this. 142

Keeping Oneself Motivated via Creative Activities.............................. 144

Instruments that are Useful for Creative and Innovative Thinking... 146

Creativity and innovation in common place activities......................... 147

Section Eleven: Financial Mastery for the Future 149
    Unexpected Events and Their Implications 150
    Financial Growth Strategies 153

Section Twelve: The Spiritual Dimensions 157
    Resilience Using Spiritual Techniques 158
    Drive from a Greater Goal 159
    Including spirituality in regular life 160
    The transforming influence of spirituality 162
    Your Peace and Purpose 166

Final Thoughts Your Straight Road 167
    Main Takeaways 168
    Get Unbreakable 169
    Your Trip Starts Now 170
    An infinitely potential life 170
    Your Perfect Life to Come 171

About The Author 173

THE UNBREAKABLE MINDSET INTRODUCTION

What does "unbreakable" mean? Indestructibility is about resilience, flexibility, and progress rather than invulnerability or avoiding difficulties. To develop a harmonious lifestyle where challenges become opportunities and failures become stepping stones to achievement, you must master the interwoven components of your mind, body, and life.

Realizing that you can influence your life is the first step towards being indestructible. Your trajectory is ultimately determined by your ideas, habits, and actions, even if outside factors may impact you. This book is your travel companion—a manual for realizing your full potential, striking a balance, and living the life you deserve.

Why This Trip Is Important

Today's fast-paced, sometimes chaotic environment might leave you exhausted, disoriented, or confused. Many people react to life without a clear goal or direction. Despite these obstacles, fantastic change is possible. Built on arranging your activities around your goals, prioritizing your physical health, and building mental strength. Think about overcoming problems with courage and commitment, not fear. Imagine living with drive, clarity, and purpose.

Being indestructible does not guarantee that you will never face difficulties. Instead, it implies that you will acquire the skills to deal with life's uncertainties graciously, becoming stronger with each failure.

What to anticipate

This book isn't about making superficial or fast improvements. Building a foundation that endures throughout time will enable you to prosper despite obstacles. We will examine five key pillars:

1. Understanding the tremendous power of your ideas and feelings and knowing how to use them for personal development is known as "mastering your mind."
2. Building a robust, healthy physique that supports your objectives and improves mental clarity is "mastering your body."
3. Finding balance, setting meaningful goals, and forming productive routines are necessary to master your life.
4. Mastering Your Environment: Creating spaces that motivate and excite you while encouraging creativity and concentration.
5. Creating a legacy that embodies your ideals, accepting change, and dedicating yourself to continual learning are all components of controlling your future.

Each chapter will provide resources, relevant information, and practical ideas to assist you on your path. We'll work together to discover the keys to leading an incredibly fulfilling and indestructible life.

The Value of Mental Capabilities

Your ideas control your life. It affects how you think about the world, make decisions, and behave. Learning to control your thoughts, emotions, and reactions is necessary for mental mastery.

This means cultivating awareness, mental toughness, and optimism. With mental mastery, you can handle life's ups and downs with confidence, composure, and clarity.

The Value of Being Able to Control Your Body

Your body serves as your means of transportation throughout life. Its maintenance is essential for physical and mental wellness. Mastering it requires good habits, exercise, and attention to your body.

A strong, healthy body and a sharp mind Help you overcome obstacles and accomplish objectives. The unbreakable attitude links physical and mental health.

Take Charge of Life Benefits

Controlling life means controlling destiny. Setting goals, preparation, and adhering to your approach are necessary.

Maintaining relationships, work, fun, and self-improvement demands balance.

Mastering your life gives you meaning and direction, especially in difficult times. This sense of mastery doesn't come from perfection but intentionality and a commitment to growth.

Holistic Living

The unbreakable mindset goes beyond toughness. We want a balanced lifestyle, mental power, and physical wellness. Mastering mind, body, and life makes you powerful, adaptable, and unstoppable.

This book will help you become indestructible by giving you the skills and tactics to succeed in all areas of life.

We Begin

Turn these pages, knowing you are capable of doing extraordinary things. Little everyday activities lead to change. The trip begins right here, right now. Enter now your ideal life shared.

SECTION ONE

IMPROVED UNDERSTANDING

Everybody's life is molded by their ideas, which affect their conduct and choices. To master ideas, one must first understand their capabilities and learn to utilize them methodically.

By taking charge of your ideas, you can influence your reality, overcome challenges, and boldly pursue your objectives. This expertise allows you to negotiate life's difficulties clearly and resolutely. Understanding your mind and developing resilience and flexibility, especially during difficult situations, are more important than repressing unpleasant feelings or constantly trying to be optimistic.

Recognizing Your Mental Power

Your brain is a sophisticated and robust machine that works on two interrelated levels—awareness and the subconscious. The secret to realizing your potential and accomplishing your objectives is comprehending how these two levels work and aligning them.

The Mind That Is Conscious

Your active, thinking mind is known as the conscious mind. It processes the information you receive from your environment, analyzes situations, makes decisions, and solves problems. This is the part of your mind that engages when you're:

- Choosing what to eat for dinner.
- Solving a math problem.
- Planning your day or strategizing for a project.

Characteristics of the Conscious Mind

- It operates in the present moment, focusing on immediate tasks and challenges.
- It works slower, requiring focus and mental energy to perform tasks effectively.
- It works slower, requiring focus and mental energy to perform tasks effectively.

The Subconscious Mind surfaces, storing habits, beliefs, memories, and emotions. It functions automatically, influencing your actions and reactions without requiring conscious thought. This is the part of your mind that:

- It guides you to brush your teeth every morning without thinking about it.
- Triggers a nervous reaction in social situations if you've had past negative experiences.
- Drives automatic responses, such as fear, excitement, or comfort in certain circumstances.

Features of the Subconscious Mind: It is emotional and habitual, depending on deeply rooted patterns. It works at breakneck speed, processing enormous volumes of information simultaneously. Training, recurrent thinking patterns, and past experiences shape it.

Aligning the Mind: To achieve your objectives and fully use your mind's power, you must ensure that your conscious and subconscious thoughts are in harmony. To achieve this alignment, you must identify and retrain limiting beliefs, cultivate empowered thinking patterns, and continuously act in ways that support them.

Subliminal Beliefs That No Longer Serve You

Step 1: Jot down recurrent thoughts or feelings in challenging situations. Patterns often reveal underlying beliefs. Many limiting beliefs are based on past experiences or societal conditioning, and they usually operate below your awareness, subtly influencing your decisions and behaviors. Think about it: What beliefs are preventing me from moving forward? For instance, I'm not good enough, or success is too difficult to attain. Feedback: Trustworthy friends or mentors can provide information about attitudes or behaviors you might not know.

Step 2: Replace Limiting Beliefs with Empowering Patterns Once identified, these limiting beliefs must be intentionally replaced with positive, empowering ones

Techniques for Reprogramming Your Mind

Affirmations

- Craft affirmations that reflect the mindset you want to adopt.
- Example: Replace *I always fail* with *I learn and grow from every experience*. Repeat these affirmations daily, ideally in the morning or before sleep when your subconscious is most receptive.

Visualization

- Spend 5–10 minutes daily visualizing yourself succeeding.

Consider its effect, appearance, and sensation. Visualization strengthens motivation and confidence by generating a mental blueprint for achievement.
- Consistent Action: Adhere to your new ideas with little, intentional action. Mental patterns are solidified by action. For example, if you believe *I am capable* Of public speaking, first practice before a mirror. Then, progress to speaking in front of a small group.

Example: Emma, an aspiring entrepreneur, struggled with the belief *I'm not smart enough to run a business.* By identifying this belief, crafting the affirmation *I am resourceful and capable of learning anything I need,* and taking actionable steps like enrolling in a business course, she gradually reprogrammed her mind for success.

Building Mental Resilience

Mental resilience is the ability to recover quickly from setbacks and persevere with a strong will. It's a talent you can acquire with deliberate effort; it's not something you're born with. Resilience strengthens your capacity to confront obstacles with clarity and confidence.

1. Engage in constructive self-talk. Your mental toughness is shaped by the words you choose to describe yourself. Positive self-talk promotes development and confidence, while negative self-talk feeds dread and self-doubt.

Strategies for Enhancing Self-Talk

- Get aware of things. Observe your self-criticism. Kindly focus on words like I cannot or *I always fail.*

- **Challenge Negative Thoughts**: Ask yourself, *Is this thought proper? What evidence supports or contradicts it?*
- **Reframe Your Words**: Replace criticism with encouragement. Example: Change: *I'll never be good at this*, but *improve with every* work.

For instance, Jacob, who often believed I was awful at presentations, started changing how he spoke to himself, including, "I'm learning to present effectively." His performance and self-assurance have increased with time.

2. Focus on Appreciation: Being grateful is a great way to change your perspective from pessimism to optimism. It assists you in maintaining your focus on the good, even in trying situations.

Be grateful:

- Take five minutes daily to write down three things you are thankful for. Examples of these are a delicious dinner, a buddy who is encouraging, or a beautiful morning.
- Consider why these things are important and how they enhance your well-being.

Impact: Research shows that regular acts of gratitude increase resilience, reduce stress, and increase enjoyment.

3. Boost Your Problem-Solving Capacity

Resilient people perceive challenges as puzzles to be solved, not as roadblocks. Developing your problem-solving ability can help you approach difficulties boldly and creatively.

Increase your capacity for problem-solving

Separate It: Sort complex problems into more manageable chunks, more doable actions.

- Example: If you feel overburdened by a large project, make a timetable or checklist.

Focus on the Solutions: Rather than worrying about the problem, focus on potential solutions.

Take Action: Start with the initial step, No matter how little. The activity decreases anxiety and increases momentum. For instance, Lily divided the project into daily assignments when she had a tight deadline at work.

4. Build a Support Network

Nobody ever achieves success by himself. A solid support system offers inspiration, perspective, and encouragement during difficult times.

How to Establish and Preserve Relationships of Support:

- **Look for Good Influences**: Be in the company of individuals who motivate, inspire, and support you.
- **Be Open:** Talk to mentors, family members, or trustworthy friends about your objectives and challenges.
- **Join Communities:** Join organizations that share your

interests, such as support groups, hobby clubs, or professional networks.

For instance, Alex's mentor helped him interpret his job loss as a chance to further his professional development. Their encouragement and coaching kept him motivated as he adjusted.

5. Take Care of Yourself

Self-care shapes resilience: it is not a luxury. Attend to your psychological, emotional, and physical needs. Needs will help you to be strong and resilient enough to meet the challenges of daily life directly.

The Force of an Aligned and Resilient Mind

cultivating resilience and mental alignment go hand in hand. You may achieve your goals and create a satisfying life when your conscious and subconscious thoughts are in sync, and you have the resources to overcome hardship.

Although this technique calls for deliberate effort, with experience, you'll discover that you can handle life's obstacles with courage and clarity. Your greatest ally is your intellect; taking care of it will lead you to an indestructible life.

Overcoming Negative Thoughts

Your potential may be limited, and negative ideas may cloud your mind; it would appear to be an endless roadblock. Traumatic experiences, anxiety, or firmly ingrained habits may all set off a vicious cycle that affects your emotions, decisions, and overall well-being. To gain control of your thoughts, you must learn to identify, challenge, and reinterpret these bad thinking habits and live an indestructible life.

It's critical to identify negative thoughts, understand the underlying reasons, and swap them out with constructive ones to overcome negative thoughts.

The Nature of Negative Ideas

People often have negative thoughts. They usually result from the anxiety that one won't live up to expectations, known as the dread of failure.

- Self-doubt: doubting your worth or abilities.
- Comparing your accomplishments to that of others is known as comparison.
- Past Experiences: Preserving unpleasant experiences that influence your opinions.

Unchecked, these ideas may result in:

- Heightened worry and stress.
- Reduced confidence in oneself.
- Restricted capacity to pursue objectives or take risks.

Fortunately, negative thinking habits are temporary. You may learn to concentrate on good things, empowering perspectives with deliberate effort.

Steps to Overcoming Negative Thoughts

1. Cultivate Awareness

To start conquering negative ideas, you must first recognize when they arise. You cannot change what you're unaware of.

How to Cultivate Awareness

- Journaling: Record your thoughts daily and note any negative patterns. Unconscious beliefs are brought to light by this exercise.
- **Mindfulness**: Pay attention to your internal dialogue without judgment. Meditation or quiet reflection helps you observe your thoughts objectively.

Example: If you frequently think, *I'm not good enough,* journaling may reveal that this thought arises when you face further difficulties or criticism. Awareness enables you to handle the sources of the notion.

2. Question the Ideas

Some bad attitudes result from presumptions or misinterpreted ideas. Face these concepts squarely to investigate their veracity and free your mind.

How do we combat negativity?

- Review the data. Consider if it is relevant this concept draws on fact or supposition.
- **Consider Alternative Perspectives**: What would a supportive friend or mentor say about this thought?
- Change the Thought to a more reasonable, helpful one.

For instance, question your belief that I will never be successful by pointing out prior successes and reinterpreting them: Success takes time, and I am making daily progress.

3. Change Your Perspective

Reframing helps you to see chances and advancement instead of restrictions.

Methods of Reframing

- **Turn Problems into Opportunities:** Instead of seeing setbacks as opportunities to develop and learn rather than as barriers,
- Replace negative thoughts with affirmations that reflect your desired mindset.

Example: Replace I always fail with I learn and improve with every experience.

4. Practice Gratitude

Gratitude helps you pay more attention to the positive aspects of your life than the negative. It's a good way to fight negativity and foster optimism.

How to Incorporate Thankfulness

- Make a list of three things for which you are thankful every day.
- Think about the reasons you care about these things.

Example: When feeling overwhelmed by work, focus on

gratitude for supportive colleagues, meaningful tasks, or the opportunity to grow professionally.

5. Limit Negative Influences

Your surroundings have a big impact on how your thoughts. Surrounding yourself with negativity through relationships, media, or habits can reinforce negative thought patterns.

How to Reduce Negative Influences

- Rate Relationships: Spend more time with upbeat folks.
- Avoid media that makes you question or dread yourself.

Emphasize educational and uplifting materials.

Create good habits by substituting creative interests or physical activity for lazy surfing or overanalyzing.

6: cultivate a resilient attitude

Resilience is the ability to bounce back from adversities. Negative long-term effects seldom influence strong brains.

To develop resilience,

- Focus on solutions rather than concentrating on problems and investigating solutions.
- **Celebrate Small Wins:** To remain happy and recognize even little development.

- **Stay Present:** Don't focus on mistakes or the future. Being present calls for mindfulness.

7. Get Help When Necessitous

Negative thoughts cannot be eliminated by you working alone. Professional counselors, trustworthy friends, or mentors might provide insightful direction and motivating support.

Look for Support

- **Tell them how you feel**: Discussing your difficulties might enable you to get peace and clarity.
- **Participate in worthwhile communities.** Spend time with others who are either facing your issues or aspirations.
- **Regarding professional direction**, Therapists and coaches might provide tactics and abilities to assist in reframing negative concepts.

Sarah's Story

"I'm not talented enough to succeed in this industry," was a persistent thought that haunted a graphic designer pursuing high-profile assignments because of this hostility. Through writing, she discovered that this idea resulted from being criticized.

To get over that, she

1. **Challenged the Thought**: She reminded herself of positive client feedback and successful projects.

2. **Her Perspective Changed:** She recognized how my unique abilities benefit every project.
3. **Practiced Gratitude:** She listed three aspects of her profession she values daily, including learning and creative flexibility.

Sarah gained confidence, allowing her to take on additional duties and grow with her business.

Important Takeaways

Overcoming negative thoughts is an ongoing process that requires awareness, persistence, and effort. You may cultivate an attitude that supports your objectives and well-being by identifying harmful habits, challenging their validity, and replacing them with empowered alternatives.

Your ideas shape your world. Mastering them is one of the most effective ways to live an indestructible existence.

Emotional and Mental Intelligence

Mental mastery involves mindfulness and EI to create a balanced, resilient, and emotionally healthy mind. They assist in managing issues. Emotions and form meaningful connections rapidly.

- **Mindfulness** keeps you anchored in the present moment, fostering awareness and calm in a world of distractions.
- If you possess emotional intelligence, you can develop

connections, recognize and control your feelings, and empathize with others.
- Living an indestructible life requires mastering these two abilities.

Staying Grounded

Being attentive entails paying attention to the present moment without making judgments.

The Benefits of Mindfulness

Reduces Stress

- Mindfulness helps regulate the stress response by activating the parasympathetic nervous system, promoting relaxation and calm.

Enhances Focus

- Mindfulness reduces distractions and improves concentration by training your mind to stay in the present.

Boosts Emotional Resilience

- Being mindful enables you to pay attention to your feelings. Without being overwhelmed, making navigating challenges easier.

How to Practice Mindfulness

1. **Mindful Breathing**

    - Spend 2–5 minutes focusing on your breath.
    - Inhale deeply through your nose, hold for a moment, and exhale slowly. Take note of how air comes into and goes out of your body.

2. **Body Scan Meditation**

    - Lie down or sit comfortably. Gradually bring your attention to each part of your body, from your toes to your head, noticing tension or sensations.

3. **Mindful Observation**

    - Choose an object (e.g., a flower, a candle flame) and observe it closely for 1–2 minutes. Focus on its details—color, texture, movement—without judgment.

4. **Mindful Walking**

    - As you walk, listen to the noises around you, the rhythm of your footfall, and the sensation of the earth under your feet.

4. **Keeping a journal**

    - Write down your emotions and ideas for five to ten minutes without editing or passing judgment. This exercise improves clarity and self-awareness.

Example: Maria, a teacher, started practicing mindfulness to manage work stress. Dedicating 10 minutes each morning to mindful breathing and reflection made her feel calmer and more focused throughout her day, even during challenging moments.

Navigating Emotions and Relationships

A person with emotional intelligence (EI) can recognize, understand, and control emotions. Your own emotions while being aware of and influencing those of others. Emotional intelligence (EI) is essential for leadership, personal growth, and successful relationships.

The Components of Emotional Intelligence

1   Self-Awareness

- The capacity to identify and comprehend your feelings, triggers, and how they affect your thoughts and behavior.
- Practice: Every day, consider your feelings. What am I experiencing, you ask? Why am I experiencing these emotions?

2   Self-Regulation

- The ability to control impulsive reactions and respond thoughtfully.
- Practice practicing deep breathing or pausing before reacting to emotionally charged events.

3. **Motivation**

    - Natural will to achieve goals and persevere against hardship.
    - Set clear goals and remind yourself of your "why" to be strong and focused.

4. **Compassion**

    - The capacity to identify with and grasp the emotions of other people.
    - Practice: Listen attentively to people, affirm their feelings, and then explore them with open-ended questions to discover their viewpoints.

5. **Social Interactions**

    - Capacity to create and maintain close ties, have good communication, and control problems.
    - Practice active listening, show thanks, and look for win-win solutions for problems.

Develop Emotional Intelligence

1. **Engage in introspection**

    - Think back on how you felt in response to different events. What set off your feelings, and how usually do you respond?

2. **Ask for comments**

- Ask mentors, coworkers, or close friends for frank comments about managing emotions and relationships.

3. **Develop empathy**

- Do perspective-taking activities. Consider, for example, the possible feelings someone else may have under a trying situation.

4. **Boost Interference**

- Give straightforward, polite communication top priority. Express your feelings using "I" words; for example, I am annoyed when deadlines are missed, as it affects my job load.

5. **Develop Conflict Resolving Skills**

- View arguments from the standpoint of addressing problems. Stay calm, pay great attention, and search for mutually beneficial outcomes.

For instance, manager John saw regular conflict among his staff. He established more supportive surroundings by raising his emotional intelligence—especially empathy and communication. This built team cooperation and confidence.

The combination of emotional intelligence and mindfulness

Mindfulness improves self-awareness, which is a key aspect of emotional intelligence.

- You may better understand yourself by focusing on your feelings and living in the present.
- Self-regulation is aided by mindfulness, which enables you to take a moment to consider your answers before responding on impulse.
- Emotional intelligence improves your mindfulness practice by strengthening relationships and encouraging improved interactions with others.

Example in Action: a sales professional, Sarah managed her nervousness before a meeting by practicing mindfulness. She was able to approach meetings with poise and tranquility because she paid attention to her breathing and objectively examined her emotions. She was able to relate to the worries of her customers thanks to her emotional intelligence, which strengthened their bonds and improved her chances of making purchases.

Benefits of Emotional Intelligence and Mindfulness

1. Better Relationships

- Being present and emotionally aware strengthens personal and professional connections.

6. Improved Ability to Make Decisions

- Emotional intelligence and mindfulness enable you to consider logic and feelings equally while making choices.

7. **Increased Sturdiness**

    - Effective emotion management helps you focus on your objectives and bounce back from failures faster.

8. **Enhanced Efficiency**

    - While emotional intelligence (EI) promotes cooperation and teamwork, mindfulness reduces distractions and increases efficiency.

Develop Emotional Intelligence and Mindfulness

1. **Start Small**

    - Set aside five to ten minutes daily for mindfulness activities, extending the time as you feel more at ease.

9. **Have patience**

    - It takes time to develop these abilities. Continue to be consistent and acknowledge minor victories.

10. **Look for Resources**

    - Additional information and techniques may be found in mindfulness and emotional intelligence books, podcasts, and workshops.

11. **Practice Every Day**

    - From practicing empathy in talks to engaging in

mindful breathing during commutes, incorporate mindfulness and emotional intelligence into your everyday life.

Mindfulness and emotional intelligence turn abilities that benefit any aspect of your life into transformational ones. You create the foundation for a strong, calm, and happy existence by paying close attention to the here and now and regulating your emotions.

The Authority of a Master Mind

Mastering your mind will help you confidently negotiate life's demands. Resilience becomes natural, negative ideas lose their hold, and emotional intelligence improves relationships.

This road calls for constancy, patience, and self-compassion. But each little action will make you stronger, more focused, and more ready to face whatever life offers.

Mental control is the foundation of an unbroken lifetime. Allow this to be the initial step towards boundless potential release.

SECTION TWO

DEVELOPING YOUR BODY

Your body is your most precious tool; it is the ship you will go through throughout every event, every obstacle, and every success. To master your body is about developing a close relationship between your mental and physical condition. And emotional moods are not just about reaching physical fitness or appearing a certain way.

When you care for your body, you feed your mind, strengthen your emotional resilience, and enable yourself to boldly and vibrantly meet the demands of daily life. A well-kept, healthy physique forms the basis for confidence, clarity, and vitality to work for your objectives.

The Body-Mind Connection

Your mind and body have a complex and important interaction. They are in continual communication, impacting and mirroring one another at every instant, not only cohabiting. Achieving balance, resilience, and general well-being requires a harmonic relationship.

Your mind gains from better attention, emotional stability, and more ability to manage stress when your body is strong and healthy. On the other hand, when your body suffers—from insufficient rest, a bad diet, or lack of exercise—your mental state frequently reflects this imbalance. It shows up as tiredness, impatience, or even worry and melancholy.

Knowing the mind-body link lets you approach your health holistically, seeing that tending one area always helps the other.

The Mind-Body Connection

The gut-brain axis is among the most well-researched instances of the mind-body link. Often referred to as your "second brain," your gut is home to billions of bacteria that generate neurotransmitters such as serotonin, dopamine, and GABA, which control mood, concentration, and rest.

The Gut-Brain Axis

- The stomach generates about 90% of the serotonin in the body, a neurotransmitter essential for mood control.
- **Gut Microbiota:** A healthy gut microbiota helps to maintain mental clarity and emotional well-being. Stress, bad food, disease, or other factors upsetting gut microbes may all contribute to mental health issues like anxiety and sadness.
- **Stress and GI System:** Often causing symptoms like bloating, cramps, or indigestion, chronic stress affects gut motility and digestion. This bodily unpleasantness then aggravates mental stress.

An illustration of this in action

Imagine a day when you ate a fast-food meal, missed breakfast, and drank minimal water. By mid-afternoon, you might feel distracted, lethargic, or agitated. Imagine a day when you began with a nutrient-dense smoothie, ate a filling meal high in protein and fiber, and kept hydrated. The change is real; your thinking feels keen, your attitude is more balanced, and you are more suited to meet obstacles.

How Physical Health Impacts Mental Well-Being

1. Nutrition

A diet high in complete, nutrient-dense meals supplies the building blocks for hormones and neurotransmitters that control mood and cognition.

Foods to Add: Salmon, walnuts, and flaxseeds include omega-3 fatty acids supporting brain function and lowering inflammation.

- Leafy greens—spinach and kale—are high in folate and linked to a better mood.
- Probiotics—yogurt, kefir, sauerkraut—promote a good gut flora.

2. Exercise

- Physical exercise boosts blood flow to the brain, supplying oxygen and nutrients vital for mental clarity.
- Exercise lowers cortisol levels, the stress hormone, and releases endorphins, a natural mood booster.

For instance, a 30-minute brisk walk improves cardiovascular health and leaves one feeling energetic and focused, lowering stress and anxiety.

3. Good quality sleep

- It helps your brain absorb memories and emotions,

strengthening resilience and emotional equilibrium. Conversely, sleep deprivation compromises emotional control, concentration, and judgment.

How Mental Health Affects Physical Attractiveness

The mind guides the body rather than responds to it. Your mental condition influences your physical condition.

1. One of the effects of chronic stress is the secretion of cortisol, which, in excess, may cause severely reduced immunological function.

2. Emotional Regulation and Physical Pain: Unresolved emotional trauma frequently shows up physically as gastrointestinal problems, muscular tightness, or headaches.

For instance, someone under significant work-related stress can have stomach trouble or tension headaches. Often, the physical symptoms go away when they are used to mindfulness or therapy to help with the stress.

Strategies to deepen the mind-body connection

1. Mindful Eating: Focus on your meals and enjoy every piece free from other distractions.

Emphasize how food affects your mood to guide your decisions on how best to feed your body and mind.

2. Combine Movement: Choose from yoga, dance, or hiking, among other physical pursuits you like. The movement should be a celebration of your body, not a job.

3. Methods include progressive muscle relaxation, meditation, and deep breathing, which help to relax the neurological system and lower cortisol levels.

4. Keep Hydrated: Dehydration affects cognitive ability and energy level. Get in the habit of regularly drinking water throughout the day.

5. Give Rest and Recovery top priority. Plan downtime to refuel mentally and physically. Enough rest enhances emotional stability and promotes general health by helping one concentrate.

Practical Use in Real Life

Case Research: Busy businessman Mark suffered from anger and persistent tiredness. Following his knowledge of the mind-body link, he made little but important adjustments:

- He substituted a nutrient-dense smoothie for his daily coffee.
- Started scheduling 15-minute mindfulness breaks throughout the day, including nighttime yoga sessions, to help with relaxation and better sleep.

Mark noticed more energy, better attention at work, and an apparent change in attitude within weeks.

The Road Towards Harmony

Learning the mind-body link can help establish a harmonic relationship between your mental and physical well-being, not just enhance your physical condition. This relationship is an excellent weapon for improving emotional balance, resilience, and attention span.

You start toward a more balanced, powerful existence when you realize how much your body and mind affect one another. Using deliberate practices and a comprehensive approach, you may lay a basis of harmony supporting your path toward unbreakability.

Diet for Ideal Health

Food is the pillar of your physical and mental health; it is more than simply food. Your energy level, attention, mood, and general health directly relate to the nutrients you eat. A well-balanced diet is about encouraging your body with the nutrients it requires to flourish, not about limitation.

Learning nutrition calls for a deliberate approach with an eye on quality, diversity, and awareness. Balanced eating habits can improve mental and physical performance, setting the basis for a lively, healthy existence.

1. Ideas for Consistent Diet

A balanced diet gives your body the necessary components to run as it should. Emphasizing premium, nutrient-dense meals can help ensure your body and mind are ready to meet the rigors of everyday living.

Whole Goods

- Give priority to unprocessed, nutrient-dense foods

such as fresh fruits, vegetables, lean meats, whole grains, legumes, and nuts; these foods contain vitamins, minerals, and antioxidants that promote cellular health, boost immunity, and improve cognitive function.
- Avoid highly processed foods. Those heavy in synthetic additives with names you cannot pronounce, unhealthy fats, and extra refined sugars usually have little nutritional value and could lower mood or energy.

For a nutrient-dense breakfast that keeps you active, substitute oatmeal topped with fresh berries and almonds for sugary cereals.

Healthy Fats

- **Brain health, lower inflammation, and support** of heart function all depend on healthy fats.
- Add omega-3 fatty acids from walnuts, flaxseeds, salmon, avocados and chia seeds.
- To support general health, include monounsaturated fats from olive oil, avocados, and almonds.

To quickly increase your consumption of good fats, include a few walnuts in your daily snack schedule or sprinkle olive oil over salads.

Hydration

- From controlling temperature to boosting cognitive functioning, almost every body's process depends on water.

- Reduced physical endurance, mental confusion, and tiredness may all result from dehydration.
- Introduce green juices and coconut water, and aim for 8–10 glasses of water daily, varying according to climate and degree of exercise.

Store a reusable water bottle to stay hydrated. Handy all day.

2. Conscious Eating Methods

Mindful eating is about raising awareness throughout meals so you may completely appreciate your food and choose better options.

Pay Attention

- Avoid distractions such as TV, cell phones, or multitasking during meals.
- Give your food's textures, tastes, and smells top priority. This habit increases pleasure and helps one avoid overindulgence.

For instance, leave your work to have lunch free from interruptions.

Portion Control

- Eat gradually so your brain has time to communicate when you are full; serve smaller amounts to prevent overindulgence.
- To automatically reduce portion sizes, use smaller plates or bowls.

Start with fewer portions and return for seconds should you still be hungry.

Know Your Body

- See how various meals impact your mood and energy level.
- Track meals and their effects to see which foods satisfy you and which could make you uncomfortable or lethargic.

For instance, add more protein or veggies to steady your energy if a high-carb meal exhausts you.

3. Successful Meal Planning

Making ahead-of-time plans and meal preparation guarantees that, even in hectic periods, you always have healthy alternatives.

Investigate Meal Prep Time

- Plan, shop, and make home-cooked meals two or three days a week.
- Easily reheatable batch-cooked foods such as soups, stews, grilled chicken, or roasted vegetables.

For instance, grill a tray of seasonal veggies on Sunday while a big pot of quinoa is boiling. Base salads, grain bowls, or side dishes on them throughout the week.

Add to a Rainbow of Foods

- One easy approach to make sure you're receiving a

good range of nutrients is with a vibrant plate.
- Fruit and vegetable colors reflect certain phytonutrients that support the body. As in: Red, tomato, and strawberry: high in lycopene, an antioxidant. Green—spinach, broccoli—packed with vitamins A, C, and K. Orange—carrots, sweet potatoes—high in beta-carotene for eye health.

Try to have it in at least three colors at every meal.

Pro Tip: Start a food journal.

Maintaining a dietary diary for one week may transform your life. One should apply this as follows:

- List everything you eat and drink.
- Note how you feel later—energy, mood, concentration, or discomfort.
- Search for trends. For instance, if you feel slow after eating processed snacks, consider substituting fresh fruit or nuts.

For instance, after journaling, Angie discovered that having a sugary breakfast made her feel exhausted mid-morning. She then switched to a smoothie high in proteins, using chia seeds, almond milk, and spinach, which kept her going until she met Myron for lunch.

Nutrition Can Change Your Life

Developing lasting habits that feed your body and mind defines mastery of nutrition—it is not about rigid diets or deprivation. Prioritizing a balanced diet can help you notice more emotional stability and resilience, better attention and mental clarity, and consistency in your daily energy level.

Every day, you can boost your well-being by eating mindfully and deliberately. Mindful, deliberate eating helps you build the foundation for a better, more powerful life.

Exercise and fitness help build a body that moves. They are vital for mental and emotional well-being and physical health. Regular exercise improves general quality of life, lowers stress, and develops mental resilience—it does not just shape your body. Since it produces endorphins, the brain's natural mood enhancer that makes you feel more energetic, focused, and cheerful, it is a great tool for overcoming everyday challenges.

Including movement in your calendar is about selecting activities you like and creating environmentally friendly habits that fit your goals and lifestyle; it does not call for a strict training routine.

1. Types of Exercises

Various types of exercise target multiple aspects of fitness, thus maintaining your body in balance, flexibility, and strength.

Cardiovascular cardio exercise

- Aims to burn calories, boost stamina, and improve lung and heart health.
- Among the examples are running, swimming, cycling, fast walking, or dance cardio.

- **Benefits:** Cardio workouts raise general endurance, decrease blood pressure, and reduce heart disease risk.

Starting with 10 to 15 minutes of vigorous walking or cycling, increase the time and intensity progressively.

Strength training

- Helps to build muscle mass, strengthen bones, and correct posture.
- Among the examples are bodyweight workouts like push-ups and squats, weightlifting, and resistance band exercises.
- Strength training increases functional strength for metabolism during everyday tasks and helps preserve muscle as one age.

Starting with small weights or bodyweight workouts can help you acquire the correct technique before increasing intensity.

Versatility and Harmony

- **Goals:** Increase mobility, lower injury risk, and encourage leisure.
- Among examples are yoga, Pilates, tai chi, and stretching exercises.
- **Benefits:** Flexibility exercises help recuperation by releasing muscular tension and correcting posture after other kinds of exercise.

Starting tip: stretch important muscle areas five to ten minutes after training.

2. Establishing an Ecological Schedule

A regular fitness program is essential for reaping the benefits of exercise. The aim is to develop pleasant, reasonable, and durable behaviors over time.

Start Small

- To foster consistency, start with brief, doable exercises.
- For instance, commit to a 10-minute daily walk. Once this becomes second nature, progressively extend and intensify the time spent.

Mix It Up

- Incorporate activities to keep things interesting and handle many fitness components.
- For instance, alternate yoga sessions, weight training, and cardio throughout the week.

Track Development

- Set objectives, monitor your development using a fitness diary or app, and mark achievements.
- For instance, note how far your runs cover or how many push-ups you do. Seeing development throughout time increases drive.

3. Including Motion in Daily Life

You don't have to go to a gym to be active; little adjustments in your everyday schedule may have a major impact.

Bike or Walk

- To boost daily exercise, substitute walking or bicycling for quick automobile excursions.

Choose steps over elevators

- Set a timer to remind yourself to stand, stretch, or move every hour while doing sedentary work.
- For instance, do 10 squats or extend your arms and back to release tension.

Short pauses throughout your day for fast bursts of movement—a stroll around the block, a few yoga postures, or a round of jumping jacks.

As a working entrepreneur, John struggled to fit exercise into his hectic schedule. Beginning modestly, he promised to walk for fifteen minutes during lunch. Over six months, he steadily progressed to jogging and added basic bodyweight workouts like planks and push-ups. These little but continuous activities changed his energy level, sharpened his concentration, and raised his general state of health.

Movement: A Way of Life

Exercise is a lifestyle that improves general happiness, mental resilience, and physical condition—it is not simply a chore to cross off your to-do list. Regular activity helps you create a physique that is not only strong and competent but also a source of energy and pleasure.

Start small, keep constant, and never forget: movement is life. Every walk, stretch, or lift you do, invests in your unshakeable path.

Rest and Recover: The Authority of Renewal

Rest is a need, not a luxury. The body uses sleep and leisure time to heal, revitalize, and prepare for demands. A well-rested body feels more balanced, thinks clearer, and performs better.

1. Giving Sleep top priority:

- Adults must have 7–9 hours of excellent sleep every night to be most effective.
- Establish a nightly ritual with reading or meditation to let your body know it is time to relax.
- Keeping your room dark, quiet, and cold will help maximize your sleeping environment.

2. Techniques for Relaxation

- Using diaphragmatic breathing can help you to relax your nervous system.
- Starting from your toes and going upward, tense and release every muscle group in progressive muscular relaxation.
- **Guided Imagery:** To help you relax, picture a serene environment—like a forest or beach.

3. Active Reversals

- Do mild yoga or walking on rest days to boost circulation and help muscular recovery.

If sleep still eludes you, look at natural therapies such as magnesium supplements or chamomile tea; if necessary, see a doctor.

Trauma Healing: Reclaiming Your Body

Trauma leaves traces on the body as much as the psyche. Unresolved trauma might show up as various health problems, persistent tension, or exhaustion. Healing calls for working on emotional as well as physical scars.

1. recognize the link.

- Know that sometimes, your body clings to prior events in ways you may not be aware of. Healing initially comes from awareness.

2. Therapeutic Strategies

- **Somatic Therapy:** Through procedures releasing repressed trauma, reawaken your body.
- Yoga, tai chi, or meditation may assist with emotional processing and physical balance restoration.

3. Self-patience and compassion

- Healing is a process rather than a race. Treat yourself

gently and acknowledge small successes as they occur.

Maria, a trauma victim, for instance, found comfort in yoga and counseling. These techniques enabled her to recover her power and agency, relax, and reconnect with her body.

The Authority of Physical Mastery

Mastery of your body is not about following social norms or aiming for perfection. Rather, it's about building a strong, healthy basis to help you overcome obstacles, follow your dreams, and have a vivid, happy life. By deliberately caring for your body, you have the energy, resilience, and clarity needed to flourish in all spheres of your life.

Your body is your best friend; it is the vehicle you will use to negotiate the highs and lows of life. Treating it with purpose, respect, and care releases its potential and helps you live completely and freely.

Constructing a strong basis

To manage your body, emphasize four fundamental pillars: conscious eating, consistent activity, enough rest, and deliberate healing. These related components cooperate to maximize your mental and physical condition.

1. Conscious Food

What you feed your body directly affects its performance and sensation. A nutrient-dense diet promotes long-term health and supplies the energy you need to get through your day.

- **Fuel for Success:** Whole, unprocessed meals boost cellular level nourishment, improving attention, mood, and stamina.
- Mindful eating is empowering via choice—paying attention to what, when, and how you eat so that your health objectives line up.

For a busy day, for example, you can substitute a handful of nuts and fresh fruit for idly chewing chips to maintain your energy and increase your focus.

2. Constant Movement

Keeping physical strength, flexibility, and endurance requires consistent movement. However, rather than being a tool of physical training, exercise is a route toward mental clarity and emotional equilibrium.

- **Strength in Motion:** Yoga or strength exercise develops resilience, arming the body to meet the rigors of everyday life.
- Physical exercise produces endorphins, which are your body's natural mood enhancer, lowering stress and improving well-being.

A quick morning stroll, for example, not only wakes your muscles but also helps you clear your mind, promoting a positive attitude for the rest of the day.

3. Enough downtime

Rest is frequently neglected, even though knowing your body

is a cornerstone. Quality sleep and leisure help one recover, become energized and maintain overall health.

- **Physical Recovery:** Sleep helps your body replenish and repair your muscles.
- Restful sleep promotes emotional control, memory retention, and cognitive ability.

For instance, developing a relaxing evening ritual—such as reading or meditating—tells your body it's time to relax, which promotes more restful sleep.

4. Healing intentionally

Your experiences—physical as well as emotional—weigh your body. By addressing prior trauma, injuries, or imbalances, intentional healing techniques help your body to operate at its best.

- Massage therapy, acupuncture, or physiotherapy are holistic treatments that help relieve stress, boost circulation, and soothe pain.
- Mind-body techniques like yoga or tai chi promote inner serenity by helping one to process and release repressed emotions.

For instance, planning frequent yoga classes or mindfulness exercises might bring energy and balance back after a time of great stress.

Considering Your Body

Learning your body calls for a close relationship to its signals and requirements, not just for organized routines. Your body speaks via hunger, tiredness, stress, and energy level changes. Understanding these signals will help you to react deliberately and with caution.

How to Listen to Your Body

- **Regularly check-in.** Stop throughout the day to evaluate your mental and physical state.
- **React kindly.** If your body communicates tiredness, give rest a priority. If it seeks movement, stretch or stroll.
- **Honor Your Restricted Capacity.** Overdoing it might cause burnout or injuries. Recover from effort in balance.

To release stress in your shoulders from work, for example, stretch or learn deep breathing.

Empowering Yourself via Mastery

Learning your body creates a partnership that will enable you to realize your aspirations. This emancipation results not from perfection but from balance and purpose.

- **Improved vitality:** A well-fed, rested body gives you the endurance to follow your interests.
- Regular activity and restorative techniques strengthen your capacity to manage stress and meet obstacles.

- Knowing you are looking after your body helps you to develop self-confidence and certainty.

For instance, take Sarah, a working mother who formerly battled poor energy and worry. Giving nutritious meals a priority, exercising every day, and getting eight hours of sleep restored her vitality to excel in her career and spend time with her family.

The Road to an Unbreakable Life

It is a journey of constant bodily mastery, not a destination. It's about valuing the process, learning from errors, and noting development.

- See your body as your friend rather than a barrier.
- Approach health with inquiry and compassion instead of pressure or judgment.
- Acknowledge that every little, good habit adds to a better, healthier you.

Your body is your life's companion, driving you toward an indelible existence. You create the basis for a life lived totally and boldly by feeding it with thoughtful nourishment, moving it with purpose, resting it with care, and mending it with compassion.

SECTION THREE

LEARNING ABOUT YOUR LIFE

Every choice you make is a stroke contributing to the painting of your life. Not perfection or strict control; learning to govern your life is about purposefully linking your actions with your values, objectives, and interests. It's about deliberately living a life in which every day advances you toward the goal you have set for yourself.

Mastering your life helps you welcome the ability to choose. Every choice becomes a chance to mold your destiny, and every habit becomes a building block for the legacy you want to produce. This process calls for clarity, equilibrium, and a dedication to living with intention.

The Authority of Intention Living

You must first understand that you are the architect of your life if you want to manage it. Though outside events may influence your path, your thoughts, actions, and beliefs determine its final course.

Goal Count

Living with intention goes beyond autopilot and requires choices based on your underlying principles. It helps you clear distractions, match your efforts to your objectives, and prioritize what matters.

For instance, suppose you get up daily with a specific goal, knowing that your activities complement your beliefs and hobbies. This feeling of direction helps you to turn daily activities into significant strides toward your perfect existence.

1. Establishing Emotional Objectives

Objectives provide a road map to your dreams and give life direction and organization. You have to create goals that motivate and challenge you if you want to dominate your life.

The SMART Model

Good objectives consist of the following:

- Specify exactly what you want to do.
- **Measurable:** Specify standards for monitoring development.
- **Achievable:** Set reasonable goals within your reach.
- **Relevant:** Match your ideals and long-term view with your objectives.
- **Time-bound:** Set deadlines to generate emphasis and attention.

For instance, instead of stating, "I want to get healthier," reinterpret your objective: "I will Three times a week exercise can help you lose ten pounds in three months eating balanced meals."

Splitting Objectives into Chapters

Big objectives seem daunting. Break them up into smaller, doable actions to help you advance under control.

- Great Objective: Author a book.
- Keystones: Create an outline; everyday write 500 words; finish a chapter every month.

Monitoring Development and Honoring Achievements

Analyze your development often and change your strategy as necessary. Celebrate achievements to keep inspiration, and thank you for your work.

For instance, Sarah said she wanted to start her own company. She methodically created her ideal business within a year by dividing it into weekly chores like competition research, business plan creation, and website design.

2. Creating Transformational Behaviors

Your everyday life's basis is habits. Mastery of your habits implies mastery of your days, then your future.

The Habit Loop Forms via a loop of:

- **Cue:** A stimulus starting the habit.
- **Routine:** The conduct itself.
- **Reward:** The advantages you get help to strengthen the habit.

For instance, waking up (cue) sets off brushing your teeth every morning (routine), which you then do and reinforced by fresh breath (reward).

How to Create Good Habits

1. Start small — start with little, doable adjustments. If you want to meditate every day, start with only two minutes.

2. Match new behaviors to already-existing ones or anchor old ones. For instance, meditate just after brushing your teeth.
3. Track your development with a habit tracker to see your consistency and keep inspired.
4. Celebrate Success or Reward yourself for maintaining your routines. For instance, treat yourself to a new book after thirty days of regular exercise.

Changing Bad Practices

List behaviors you no longer find useful and substitute for better choices.

- Instead of browsing late at night, read or journal.
- Replace sweet munchies with almonds or fresh fruit.

For instance, John improved his sleep quality and energy levels by substituting 20 minutes of yoga for his late-night TV viewing.

3. Effective Time Management

Your most valuable resource is time. Dominating your life means dominating your time by prioritizing what is important.

Eisenhower's Matrix

Use this tool to sort chores according to significance and urgency;

- Do them immediately.
- Plan these chores to concentrate on long-term objectives.

- They are not urgent but yet crucial.
- Eliminate these chores to save time by not urgently and not importantly squandering it.

Blocking Time

Set up certain chunks of time for particular activities. This habit guarantees concentrated working times and helps to reduce distractions.

For instance, spend 8–9 AM addressing emails, 9–11 AM working creatively, and 11–12 PM in meetings.

Task batches

Combine related chores to minimize mental tiredness and boost effectiveness.

For instance, answer all emails simultaneously rather than randomly during the day.

Learn to say no

Save time by turning down obligations incompatible with your priorities.

4. Living With Intent

The compass guiding your choices and inspiring your enthusiasm is your purpose. A purpose-driven existence is harmonic, balanced, and consistent with your ideals.

Finding Your Purpose

- Reflect on your interests, aptitudes, and the factors motivating you.
- Wonder: What makes me happy? What difference do I want to bring about?

Matching Behavior with Goal

Make sure your everyday decisions complement your long-term view. Purposive living prioritizes what counts most and let's go of what doesn't.

Changing Regularly

As you develop, your goals could change. Review your beliefs and goals often to ensure they fit your objectives.

For instance, Lisa, a business professional, realized that her calling was serving others. She changed her path to charitable work and found greater satisfaction in her efforts.

Living with Intent

Graphic designer Michael was dissatisfied even with a great job. Setting significant goals—such as broadening his skill set and launching a side project—rekindled his enthusiasm. He developed regular routines, including spending an hour every evening on his interests, and employed time-blocking to manage his job and family life. Over time, Michael freelanced, aligning his work with his principles and goals.

Your Road to Mastery of Your Life

Mastery of your life is not about striving for perfection or tightly regulating every aspect. Rather, it's about adopting a deliberate attitude in which every activity you do fits your ideals and advances you toward your objectives. It's about planning your days according to your priorities, developing habits that empower you, and choosing what speaks to your vision for a meaningful and fulfilled life.

Learning to master your life is beautiful in the journey as much as in the end. It's about realizing that every moment has the power to add to the masterwork you are producing and about owning your time and energy.

Living with Attention

Living with the aim is approaching life actively rather than passively. It's about choosing deliberately in line with your principles and long-term goals.

How to Grow Intent

1. Define Your Values Clearly

- Think back on the things that are important to you. Is family, invention, personal development, or community service?
- To help you make decisions, list your five strongest values.

2. Establish Reasonable Objectives

- List the spheres of life where you want to concentrate your time and effort.
- Let your everyday activities and long-term goals reflect these priorities.

3. Be Present

- Steer clear of multitasking and give the current work or person your whole focus.

For instance, Anna, a young professional, felt cut off from her everyday life. Clarifying her values—creativity, health, and connection—she prioritized painting, daily walks, and frequent buddy calls. This change gave her life greater happiness and meaning.

Routines for developing your everyday life help you to empower yourself. Little deeds done regularly add up over time to help decide your fate.

Methods of Establishing Empowering Actions

1. Start basic

- concentrate on one behavior at a time to reduce overburden. Little adjustments are easily maintained and have long-term effects.

2. Foundation for Present Routines

- Combine old and new events to provide a flawless transition.
- Spend five minutes of meditation, for example, after tooth brushing.

3. Record your development using a notebook or smartphone., therefore honoring milestones.

4. Accept Flexibility: If you miss a day or have to change your schedule, let yourself gracefully handle it.

For instance, John battled motivation yet desired better physical health. He began with a five-minute morning stretch, then progressively added running and muscle building. Within months, his daily schedule naturally included exercise.

Time Is Your Most Important Tool

Time is limited; your choices about how to spend it define the nature of your existence. Learning your life includes learning your time and ensuring it fits your objectives and priorities.

Tips for Practical Time Management

1. Create structure by scheduling events, appointments, and downtime using a planner or calendar.
2. Use the Eisenhower Matrix to prioritize chores according to urgency and relevance so that one may concentrate on what counts.
3. Grouping activities and batch-related tasks help boost

efficiency and lower mental tiredness.
4. Plan Downtime; rest and leisure are as important as output. Schedule time for interests, socializing, and self-care.

For instance, Michael juggled family, job, and personal pursuits. Time-blocking his week allowed him to set aside certain hours for each goal, increasing his satisfaction and output.

Designing a Life of Transparency, Harmony, and Fulfillment

Mastery of your life calls for balance rather than just intention, habits, and time management. A happy life balances leisure, relationships, career, and personal development.

How to Create Harmony

1. **Review your commitments often and periodically modify them to align with your ideals.**
2. **Learn self-compassion**; realize that equilibrium is dynamic rather than fixed. The needs of life change, so your strategy should also.
3. **Honor Development Thank you for your efforts, no matter how little**. Thanks for the trip. It will help you to be more fulfilled generally.

Every Decision Is a Paintstroke

Every choice you make, every habit you develop, every minute you spend painting on the painting of your life. The little, deliberate decisions you make every day characterize the masterwork you are producing rather than great movements or perfection.

You own the canvas to paint. Approach it fearlessly, believing that your consistent dedication to your principles and intentional actions will result in a life of beauty, purpose, and significance.

Using intentional effort and consistency, you can design a life that represents your best hopes. Start today—one decision, one habit, one moment at a time—and watch your masterwork come to pass.

SECTION FOUR

DOMINATING YOUR ENVIRONS

Your surroundings constitute the background of your existence, affecting not just the places you live but also your attitude, output, and general health condition. Setting the basis for success and personal development is deliberately creating and arranging environments that empower and uplift you, thereby controlling your surroundings.

A supportive atmosphere is a great friend; it keeps you on track with your objectives, stimulates creativity, and helps you be positive. Your surroundings—your house, place of employment, digital environment, or financial scene—should mirror and support the life you want to create.

The Effect of Your Surroundings

Your surroundings influence your mental and emotional condition. While a clean, orderly, and customized workplace promotes clarity, attention, and balance, crowded or chaotic surroundings may cause stress, overload, and distraction.

Why Is Context Important?

- A neat desk lowers distractions, therefore improving attention and output.
- Affects mindset Surroundings with positive factors inspire resilience and hope.
- Promotes wellbeing. Harmonic environments help lower stress and raise happiness.

Establishing a Positive Environment

Starting with deliberate design, ensure every place you live supports your beliefs and objectives and helps you master your surroundings.

1. Cleaning for clarity

Clutter may cause mental noise, therefore impairing concentration and ease of use. It is more than simply physical. Decluttering your surroundings helps you to be in peace and order.

Declutters Steps

- **Start small—begin with a single shelf, desk, or drawer.** Gradual improvement develops momentum and avoids overload.
- **The "Joy Test":** See if something makes you happy or fulfills a need. Should it not, give, recycle, or toss it.
- **Regular Maintenance:** Spend five to ten minutes cleaning daily to help avoid building clutter.

Pro Tip: Set aside a specific monthly decluttering day for closet, kitchen cabinet, or storage space needs.

For instance, Lisa, a writer, found that her messy desk interfered with her output. She cleaned her desk, retaining only a few inspirational objects and basic equipment. This resulted in More concentration and fresh creative inspiration.

2. Including Nature

Nature can help one relax, sharpen attention, and boost general well-being. Including natural materials in your surroundings has a calming, revitalizing effect.

Methods for adding natural elements

- **Houseplants:** Brighten your area and help to clean the air by including vegetation. Great options include easy-care plants like pothos, snakes, or succulents.
- **Natural Light:** Using sheer curtains or rearranging furniture can help to maximize natural light. Sunlight raises energy and mood levels.
- **Earthy Colors and Textures**: Use wood, stone, or spun linens in your décor to create a feeling of groundedness and peace.
- Mark, a distant worker, for instance, battled isolation. He set his desk in front of a window and added houseplants to make the workstation more inviting, lowering stress and boosting imagination.

3. Customizing Your Domain

Your surroundings should represent your moral values and character. Personalizing your surroundings can help you relax and motivate you; the surroundings will appear, especially yours.

- Showcase images of loved ones, artwork, or mementos from significant events to inspire happiness and drive in your space.

- **Vision boards and quotes:** To keep your objectives and ambitions front and center, design a vision board or exhibit inspirational quotations.
- Incorporate interests and hobbies by surrounding yourself with objects that speak to your passions, such as books, painting tools, or musical instruments.

For instance, a graphic artist, Emma, felt unmotivated at her workstation. Emma turned her desk into a creative and focused center by including a vision board with her professional aspirations, tool organization, and art she enjoyed. This shift raised her energy and output.

Learning Digital Domains

Like your actual surroundings, your digital environment has a great impact. Keeping order and intentionality in your digital environment is crucial, given how much of life is online.

Organizing Your Digital Environment: Steps

- Sort files into folders, delete pointless programs and tidy your email inbox.
- Create tech-free areas or periods to help to prevent digital overload.
- Create Your Content: Consume media aligned with your values and goals, then follow stories.

John streamlined his digital life using a task management program, desktop organization, and spam email subscription. This reduced stress and increased output.

Creating a Suitable Financial Situation

Your financial conduct shapes your environment, affecting your freedom and security. Knowing this implies creating ways to reduce your financial load and enable you to reach your goals.

Strategies for Mastering Finance

- Program automated transfers to savings or investment accounts.
- Track spending using budgeting tools to see where your money goes and make any changes.
- Pay off high-interest debt and streamline your accounts to be organized.

For instance, Sarah tracked spending using a budgeting tool and automated her monthly savings. She felt more in charge and certain about her financial future within months.

Real-Life Application: Emma's Development

A graphic artist, Emma would often be bored and sidetracked at her desk. Understanding her surroundings, she changed various things:

- Added houseplants to give her workspace freshness and vitality.
- Arrange her tools and materials for simple access.
- Designed a vision board with her preferred inspirational quotations and professional objectives.

Thanks to these few changes, her job became a creative and focused paradise, which increased her output and energy.

Your Environment as Mirror of Your Objectives

Learning to master your surroundings is about designing places that mirror and assist the life you choose to lead, not just about appearances. When your surroundings fit your goals, they provide a potent stimulus for enjoyment, creativity, and personal development.

Decluttering, adding natural components, customizing your home, and streamlining your digital and financial surroundings can help you build a world that enables you to flourish.

Daily inspiration from your surroundings should remind you of your potential and aspirations. Create a place where balance rules, creativity runs wild, and optimism blossoms.

Finding Work-Life Balance

The border separating business from personal life sometimes disappears in the highly linked world of today. Mastering your surroundings means establishing limits, guarding your time and energy, and guaranteeing harmonic parts of life.

1. Define precise limits

- Set out certain times for personal and professional pursuits. Stay within these limits to maintain harmony.
- Establish a separate workstation, even if it's only a little part of your house. This bodily difference helps your

mind move between rest and work.

2. Plan Downtime

- Mark on your calendar time for interests, family, or leisure. See this break as precious and nonnegotiable.
- Participate in energizing pursuits, including reading, walking, or hanging out with loved ones.

3. Free up your brain resources

- Use technology to automate menial chores such as meal planning or bill payment processing.

Tip: Set your gadgets on "Do Not Disturb" mode during personal time to lose yourself in the moment and prevent work disruptions completely.

Controlling Digital Distractions

Technology may cause stress and distraction, even if it has many advantages. Mental clarity and attention depend on how one manages one's digital environment.

1. One day or weekend, do a digital detox and disconnect. Spend this time re-engaging in offline pursuits such as writing or hiking.

    - Create boundaries by designating tech-free zones in your house—such as the dining room or bedroom.

2. Set timers or use limitations on your applications to limit social media use or define screen time.

   - Just check emails at scheduled intervals to prevent continual disruptions.

4. Customize Your Online Environment

   - Avoid following accounts that conflict with your objectives or saps your energy.
   - Regularly eliminate extraneous objects and arrange digital assets into well-named folders.

Applied Real-Life: Constant alerts and unending scrolling overwhelmed Mark, a marketing specialist. He enhanced his attention, slept better, and had more time for interests like painting by shutting off pointless alarms and restricting social media to thirty minutes daily.

Financial Wellness

Your physical and digital surroundings are secondary compared to your financial surroundings. Organizing and securing your money helps lower stress and provide new possibilities.

1. Make a budget

- monitor your income and expenditure to learn about your financial behavior.
- Set aside money for staples, savings, and leisure to balance needs with enjoyment.

2. Make an emergency fund

Aim to save three to six months of living expenses. This cushion provides ease of mind during unexpected events like job loss or medical problems.

3. Establish short-term financial goals

Long-term: Save for a house down payment or invest in retirement savings.

Use books, podcasts, or online courses to learn about personal finance. Information helps you to increase your riches and make wise selections.

Practical Relevance: Until Lisa began monitoring her expenses, she, a teacher, battled to save. She created financial stability in a year and felt more hopeful about her future by channeling unneeded spending into an emergency fund.

Increasing Your Mastery of the Environment

1. Your Social Scene

- Around you, surround yourself with individuals who inspire and uplift. Cut off poisonous associations that sap your vitality or impede your development.
- Interact with organizations or communities that share your beliefs and interests to help build support and a feeling of belonging.

2. Your Mental Environment

- Curate the stuff you read. Select podcasts, books, and performances that complement your objectives and sharpen your intellect.
- Thanks for helping you change your mental surroundings from negative to positive. Your Spiritual Environment

3. Your Spiritual Environment

- Whether it's a local park or a peaceful area in your house, set aside a place for meditation or introspection.
- Incorporate rites or ceremonies that speak to your ideals to anchor and refocus you.

Jacob's Story

Jacob, a software engineer, felt his surroundings constantly busy and taxing. His phone Jacob, a software engineer, felt that his surroundings were constantly busy and overwhelming. His phone bombarded him with notifications; his work was disorganized; his finances made him anxious.

Following his reading on mastering his surroundings, Jacob took action:

- He set screen time limits, unsubscribed from distracting newsletters, and created tech-free zones in his house
- He built a budget, paid off debt, and started an emergency fund.

The outcome was revolutionary. Jacob's output shot, his stress dropped, and he felt more in charge of his life than he had ever known.

The Authority of a Synced Environment

Mastering your surroundings is about building a foundation that actively supports your objectives, expresses your beliefs, and improves your general well-being—not just about keeping things neat or visually beautiful. An aligned environment shapes your attitude, output, and enjoyment and functions as both a mirror and a driver for the life you want to live.

Taking control of your surroundings means taking control of your life. Every choice about decluttering, organizing, or personalizing your area moves toward balance, clarity, and concentration. Carefully chosen surroundings help you to flourish in all spheres of your life, not just support your goals.

Align Your Objectives

1. Concentration and Efficiency

- A neat, orderly workplace reduces distractions so that you may focus on important work.
- Like clear workstations, labeled storage, and ergonomic furniture—intentional design improves comfort and productivity.

2. Emotional Well-Being

- Surrounding oneself with significant objects, natural

elements, and calming hues helps you to relax.
- A calm bedroom with little clutter and gentle lighting may help with emotional resilience and better sleep quality.

3. Value reinforcement

- Spaces reflecting your priorities help you stay aligned with your goal. Showing equipment for hobbies, inspiring sayings, or vision boards helps you to remember your goals.

Mirror of Your Values

Your surroundings tell volumes about your priorities and values. When your surroundings align with your objectives, they are a daily reminder of your aims and guide you into activities that complement them.

Value-Driven Spaces

- **Creativity:** A painter would have a bright, open studio with quick access to brushes, canvases, and paints.
- **Health:** A fitness fan can set up a home gym or have healthy foods in their kitchen.
- **Connection:** A family-oriented person may prioritize the inviting living room for events.

Change Your surroundings

Emphasize deliberate design and careful procedures to maximize the potential of an aligned environment.

1. **Curate with intention.**

   - Regularly declutter things you no longer use to make room for what does.
   - Personalize Thoughtfully: Surround yourself with meaningful family photos, travel souvenirs, or artwork that motivates drive and optimism.

2. **Methodologies for Juggling**

   - Starting every day with meditation, cleaning, or window opening to let in natural light, you will establish a positive tone.
   - **Evening Wind-Down**: Mark when you should unwind with gentle lighting, scent-based signals, or light music.

3. **Optimally Share Resources**

   - **Digital Areas:** To maintain a clean digital environment, limit alerts, manage files, and manage email inbox clutter.
   - **Financial Environment:** Simplify your money utilizing software for automated savings, budgeting tools, or streamlined bill payments to reduce stress.

The Well-Aligned Environment

Learning to master your surroundings sets off a chain reaction that affects every element of your life:

- **Enhanced Mindset:** A tranquil environment boldly

helps you face difficulties using positivism and mental clarity.
- **Improved Productivity:** Clean surroundings help one to focus and raise output by removing pointless distractions.
- **More improved Relationships:** A welcoming and peaceful home fosters stronger bonds with family members and creates opportunities for meaningful interactions.
- **Sustainable Growth:** You may regularly pursue personal development free from opposition when your surroundings help you to achieve your objectives.

Empowering Your Surroundings

Learning your surroundings is a kind of empowerment. Though it takes attention and constant work, the benefits are enormous.

Advice on Assuming Leadership

5. Start small and concentrate on one area at a time—a desk, closet, or digital folder. Progressive development helps avoid overload.
6. Adopt minimalism and keep only what improves your life. Simplicity allows creativity and clarity.
7. Set aside time every week to keep your areas in good condition and maximize them so they will always meet your changing demands.

Your surroundings as a growth-catalyst

An aligned environment actively participates in your path, not just provides a background. It prepares you for your goals, keeping you grounded, motivated, and focused.

Your surroundings should inspire rather than confine you. Taking charge of your surroundings lays a strong basis for happiness, harmony, and success. Let your environment mirror your ideals, help you toward your objectives, and enable you to lead the unbroken life you are due.

SECTION FIVE

DEVELOPING YOUR FUTURE

The future is an empty canvas ready for Your masterwork, an unbounded range of possibilities. It offers progress, challenges, and opportunities—all fashioned by the actions and intentions you choose today. Learning to master your future is about being ready with resilience, flexibility, and a clear vision rather than forecasting what is coming.

You create the basis for a happy and purposeful existence by welcoming change, pledging lifetime learning, encouraging invention, and creating a meaningful legacy. Every action toward controlling your destiny opens a road toward success, flexibility, and ongoing development.

Accepting Transformation

Among the only things definite in life is change. Although frightening or disruptive, it is also a great driver of development and evolution. You have to learn to see change as a chance to develop, adjust, and innovate rather than as a danger if you are to manage your future.

1. Developing an Open Mindset

- Change should be considered a chance to expand your horizons and probe new directions. Losing a job, for instance, might result in a career better fit for your interests.
- Welcome inquiries and tackle challenges. What might this teach me? In what ways may this situation help me to grow? Curiosity turns anxiety into research and invention.

2. Methodical Approaches for Control of Change

- **Evaluate the situation:** concentrate on the areas of the change under your influence. Accepting the unpredictable helps you to behave clearly and releases tension.
- **Go for little steps.** Sort important changes into doable tasks. If relocating to a new city seems intimidating, look at neighborhoods or contact nearby civic associations.
- **Get help;** shared change is easier. For guidance and support, consult reliable friends, mentors, or counselors.

Alex's status seemed questionable due to a significant corporate restructure. Alex actively sought out more responsibilities and showed flexibility rather than succumbing to his anxiety. He was hired and promoted due to his efforts, highlighting the value of accepting change.

Respecting ongoing learning is the lifelong journey from where you are to where you want to be. Maintaining curiosity and flexibility helps you stay relevant in a constantly changing world, creates new opportunities, and strengthens your skills and resilience.

1. Create a Learning Plan

- Specify Learning Objectives
- Leverage Resources: Use books, online courses, podcasts, and seminars to increase your knowledge in certain areas—such as learning a new language, gaining technical proficiency, or investigating artistic interests.
- Debate regular hours each week for study. Over time,

even thirty minutes a day may cause notable improvement.

2. Apply what you learn

- Use fresh information in your everyday life or at your place of employment. For your calendar, for example, utilize recently acquired time management strategies.
- Share what you learn to help your community and validate your knowledge.

3. Develop a Growth mindset

- Replace constrictive ideas like, I can't do this with, I can learn how to accomplish this.
- See losses as chances for development rather than mistakes.

In real life, this may be Sarah's promise to choose one new talent every year. She started with web design and devoted thirty minutes daily to online lessons. Two years ago, she doubled her salary and found a better work-life balance when she began a successful freelancing design profession.

Encouraging Creativity and Innovation

Creativity is a talent that helps you to solve issues, think outside the box, and realize new ideas; it is not just a talent of artists.

1. Techniques to Increase Creativity

- Freely brainstorm for ten minutes, scribbling down

every idea—no matter how unusual. This procedure opens fresh viewpoints.
- Pursue creative hobbies that stimulate new ideas: painting, writing, or instrument playing.
- Take breaks; frequently, stepping away from an issue results in discoveries. Physical activity helps you relax; examples of this include stretching or walking.

2. Promoting Creativeness

- Request "What If?" Question presumptions and weigh other strategies.
- Work with other teams to get new ideas and viewpoints.
- Accept trial and error; see every effort as a teaching moment.

A small company owner, David, conducted team brainstorming sessions to inspire innovation. This approach produced creative marketing plans that increased income by 20%, proving the value of group invention.

Developing a Legacy

A significant legacy is that which you leave behind—positive. It's about the people you influence and the world you help, not money or celebrity.

1. Describe Your Legacy

- Think about issues such as: What would I desire to be known for? How may I help others live their life?

- Match your long-term vision with your everyday activities.

2. Approaches to Create Your Legacy

- Mentoring: Share your expertise to motivate and direct others.
- Philanthropy: Donations, volunteering, or advocacy help causes connected to your interests.
- Write a book, start a community project, or set up a scholarship fund to create something enduring.

3. Live Your Legacy Every day

- Understand that big acts alone do not define your legacy. These are the little, constant acts that represent your values and character.

Real-Life Example: Retired teacher Lisa established a scholarship for less fortunate kids. Her action gave her community access to educational possibilities and motivated them to help, increasing her influence.

Making Your Life Future-Proof

Future preparation is arming you to fit changes in sectors, technology, and the living environment.

1. Keep Informed

- Follow trends in your line of work and in areas of interest.

- Join professional networks, attend seminars, and always look for learning opportunities.

2. Create Versatility

- Acquire communicative, critical thinking, and adaptable abilities. These have great value in many different sectors.
- Accept new tools and technology to remain competitive in a changing employment environment.

3. Anticipate uncertainty.

- Build financial safety nets with several income sources and emergency money.
- Create backup plans for family dynamics, professional moves, or relocation.

In real life, this may be Accountant Jennifer saw that her field depended more on technology. She kept her job and progressed into senior positions by aggressively mastering data analytics.

Constructing a Resilient and Reward Future

Learning your future is about arming oneself with the means to flourish among unpredictability, not about forecasting every turn or controlling every result. Though life is full of unanticipated events, with vision, flexibility, and purpose, you can negotiate obstacles, grab possibilities, and build a future that honors your goals.

One does not create a strong and fulfilling future overnight. It results from conscious decisions, steady development, and a will to match your behavior with your ideals. You make the basis for a happy life marked by significance and influence by welcoming change, encouraging innovation, and emphasizing the legacy you want to leave.

Resilience: Foundation of a Future Bright

Resilience is the capacity to rise from disappointments, overcome obstacles, and become stronger. It's a talent you can grow over time rather than a set quality.

Create Future Resilience

1. Flexibility to Accept change in your strategy and ideas: Realize that there is seldom a straight road to achievement and that sometimes veers result in unanticipated development.
2. Emotional Awareness: Sort and absorb your feelings. When facing difficulties, A clear mental state allows you to focus and make wise judgments.
3. Problem-Solving Techniques: Divide difficult problems into smaller, doable stages. Dealing with issues little by little lessens overwhelm and increases confidence.

Maria, for instance, spent her time learning new skills, networking, and investigating freelance prospects after losing her job during a recession. Her flexibility raised her earning capacity and helped her get a new job.

Vision - the Success Manual

A clear vision is like a lighthouse guiding your efforts and choices toward a deliberate and satisfying existence.

Writing a Vision for the Future

- Clearly state your long-term and short-term goals. In the coming year, what goal do you want to reach? The ten years to come?
- See Success or Spend time visualizing your dream future. Visualizing not only inspires but also helps you to understand the actions required to reach your objectives.
- Make a road plan and divide your vision into doable benchmarks. To launch a firm, start with industry research, business plan creation, and network development.

For instance, a budding writer named David imagined releasing his first book five years from now. He established small objectives: 500 words per day, finishing a book in two years, and finding a publisher the next year. His sharp vision kept him on target and inspired.

Aim - the Center of Contentment

Your activities have significance thanks in large part to your purpose. It's the "why" guiding your choices and aspirations.

Matching Activities with Goals

- Think about your values: family, creativity, community,

or personal development; then, let them guide your decisions.
- Discover Your Passion and Participate in joyful and energizing activities. The convergence of what you enjoy and what benefits others often determines your purpose.
- Make sure your everyday activities line up with your long-term goals. Regular, deliberate living produces a life of satisfaction.

For instance, former corporate executive Lisa discovered her calling in coaching young professionals. She matched her job with her interest by moving into a consultancy position and discovering fresh enthusiasm and gratification in her work.

The Legacy and Creativity Play

Creativity drives invention and problem-solving, helping you break free from constraints and construct a future fit for your goals. At the same time, emphasizing legacy guarantees that your life's influence goes beyond your successes.

Encouraging Originality to Support Development

- Try fresh ideas and points of view to adopt a lively attitude.
- Work with others to mix many points of view and inspire creativity.

Creating a Respected Legacy

- Share your expertise, mentor others, and keep causes consistent with your principles.

- Whether a project, a work of art, or a charitable endeavor, it produces something timeless.

For instance, retired teacher Sarah started a scholarship program for poor youngsters, fostering an educational legacy and opportunity that still inspires her neighborhood.

Acting: Your Paintbrush on the Life Canvas

The future is a blank canvas just ready for your intentional brushwork. Every deliberate choice and little action adds richness and color to the masterwork you are producing.

How To Get Started Right Now

1. **One should decide on one area of development or goal to concentrate on.** Divide it up into doable steps and start right away.
2. **Track Development**: Note your successes in a notebook or planner and consider your path forward.
3. Celebrate little victories and acknowledge and honor advancement of any kind. Acknowledging development gives one impetus and confidence.
4. **Stay Flexible.** Get ready to change your strategies as conditions develop. Oftentimes, growth calls for adapting to new chances and problems.

Your Exclusive Masterpiece

Mastering your future is a journey rather than a destination. It's about seizing control of what you can, being ready for what you cannot, and always moving toward your goals.

VICTOR IMHANS

You own the canvas to cover; the brush is in your hand. Start with one deliberate action and see how your masterwork develops vivid and full of potential.

SECTION SIX

RESILIENCE AND EMOTIONAL REGULATION DEVELOPMENT

R esilience and emotional control are the most critical skills for fulfilling everyday duties. They provide a formidable arsenal for managing tension, overcoming hurdles, and maintaining attention in stressful situations. These skills help you overcome life's challenges, promote personal development, strengthen bonds with others, and open doors to long-term success.

You may manage how you react to the environment by developing resilience and emotional mastery. By taking control of your emotional environment, you may overcome hardship with poise and resolve rather than being at the whim of outside circumstances.

The Significance of Emotional Intelligence and Resilience

The Function of Emotional Intelligence

The capacity to identify, comprehend, and manage your emotions in a manner that empowers rather than governs you is known as emotional mastery. It all comes down to staying collected under pressure and making well-considered judgments even in the most trying circumstances. Emotional mastery is properly controlling your emotions so they work for you rather than against you. It is not about repressing your feelings.

Emotions are a part of existence. They are our internal reactions to the things, people, and circumstances we encounter. Without emotional control, these instinctive reactions may become overpowering, resulting in poor judgment, rash decisions, and damaged relationships. On the other hand, when you have control of your emotions, you can cope with challenging situations with elegance, clarity, and focus.

Emotional Intelligence Benefits

Better Decision-Making: Decisions made under pressure are often reactive rather than deliberate when emotions are running high. The ability to control your feelings gives you the clarity to stop, evaluate, and make decisions consistent with your beliefs and objectives.

Consider being reprimanded at work, for instance. You might react defensively or feel defeated if you don't have emotional control. It allows you to assess the feedback's veracity objectively, disentangle the emotion from it, and utilize it to do better.

Become Stressless: By controlling your emotions, you can react to pressures with composure and control instead of allowing them to cause you to become anxious or frustrated. This protects your physical and emotional health, as long-term stress may cause problems, including decreased immunity and high blood pressure.

Example: Emotional mastery keeps you focused on solutions within a high-pressure deadline, preventing you from feeling overwhelmed by the task's size.

Emotional self-control helps one have better relationships, improved communication, empathy, and understanding.

Encouraging peace and reducing misunderstandings strengthens relationships personally and professionally.

Emotional mastery, for example, helps you to settle rather than aggravate a conflict with a loved one by enabling you to listen carefully and silently.

The Dangers of Insufficient Emotional Control

Impulsive Reactions: If you lack emotional control, you can behave impulsively out of fear, rage, or irritation and regret what you did.

For instance, yelling at a coworker during a tense meeting may harm your relationships and reputation in the workplace.

Clouded Judgment: when emotions take over, logical reasoning may be obscured, resulting in bad choices.

For instance, selling stocks during a market decline or making other significant financial decisions out of fear or worry may lead to needless losses.

Burnout on an emotional level. It may be draining to always be at the mercy of your emotions, resulting in burnout and a decreased ability to handle day-to-day difficulties.

Personal Development and Emotional Mastery

Emotional mastery is fundamental to personal development because it enables you to face life's obstacles with resilience and purpose. Understanding and controlling your emotions helps you

- **Develop Self-Awareness:** Being aware of your emotional patterns allows you to pinpoint areas where you need to develop and improve.
- **Develop Confidence:** Emotional control increases confidence in managing challenging circumstances.
- **Improve Focus:** You may focus on reaching your objectives by minimizing emotional distractions.

Example in Action: Young entrepreneur Jane was turned down after presenting her company proposal to investors. Without emotional control, she may have given in to irritation and self-doubt. Rather, she worked through her disappointment, looked for helpful criticism, and improved her presentation. At her subsequent presentation, she got money thanks to her ability to regulate her emotions.

Useful Applications of Emotional Mastery

1. **In the Workplace:** Emotional control keeps you calm and professional even in highly demanding surroundings. It improves your leadership as others find those who stay composed under duress appealing.
2. Emotional mastery helps one to improve communication, empathy, and understanding, thus strengthening more satisfying relationships.
3. **Personal Development:** Mastery of your emotions opens room for introspection and personal development. It helps you to see issues as possibilities rather than causes for anxiety by approaching them with interest.

The Value of Tenacity

Resilience is the capacity to bounce back from obstacles, adjust to change, and press on with purposeful, determined forward movement. It is not the lack of difficulty but the capacity to meet it head-on, rising wiser and stronger. Life is erratic by nature, and there are chances and problems. Resilience guarantees that challenges won't stop you from advancing but will serve as stepping stones for development and change.

Resilience is a talent that can be developed with deliberate effort and practice. It is far from a natural ability limited to a few people. Resilience helps you maintain emotional equilibrium, focus on your objectives, and find purpose even in demanding circumstances.

The Function of Resilience in Negotiating Obstacles

Changing Setbacks into Teaching Tools

Resilience lets you see obstacles or disappointments as learning moments rather than insurmountable problems. Changing your perspective will enable you to use challenges to improve your approach and focus your ideas.

For instance, Sarah utilized her experience—turned down for a promotion—as a chance to evaluate her abilities, get comments, and sign up for a leadership course instead of moping over the letdown. Her proactive approach paid off; she confidently and competently got the following promotion.

Changing with grace: Adaptation

Change is unavoidable in your personal life, job, or outside environment. Resilience lets you welcome change instead of fighting it, helps you to react fast, and choose fresh directions ahead.

For instance, Peter's job disappeared when his business was reorganized. Instead of giving up, he used his network, changed his credentials, entered another area, and landed a position fit for his interests.

Retaining emotional balance

Resilience is about correct control of emotions rather than about suppressing them. Strong people understand their feelings, assist in constructive processing, and move with clarity and intent.

Emma allowed herself time to process a sad breakup and concentrated on joyful pursuits like painting and hiking. Her ability to bounce back enabled her to approach the next partnerships from a better perspective.

Essential traits of strong individuals

1. **Optimism**: Resilient people keep a positive attitude as they think that problems are transient and that there are workable solutions.
2. **Self-awareness:** By knowing one's emotions, triggers, and mental patterns, one may react deliberately instead of responding.
3. **Adaptability**: Resilient individuals are versatile in their attitude and thinking and can handle new situations

without losing their view of their objectives.
4. **Strong Support Systems**: Developing relationships with friends, relatives, or mentors gives one hope and perspective under trying circumstances.
5. **Sense of Purpose**: Resilient people are driven to keep going despite difficulty by well-defined objectives and ideals.

Building Resilience: Useful Approaches

1. Change Challenges

See challenges as chances to improve. Ask yourself, what may I learn from this? How may this experience advance me?

2. Create constructive coping strategies.

Participate in activities that lower stress and provide balance, including meditation, writing, exercise, or natural time.

3. Create a Robust Support System

Surround yourself with upbeat, helping individuals who could provide encouragement, guidance, or a listening ear.

4. Provide reasonable objectives.

Divide big projects into smaller, doable chores to prevent feeling overburdened. Honor little victories to keep the momentum.

5. Train Thankfulness

Pay more attention to your possessions than to your lack.

Thanks, helps you to see things differently and develop a strong attitude.

An Instance of Action is a Story of Fortitude

John felt angry and demoralized after being passed over for a much-awaited promotion. Still, he resolved to direct his feelings toward good use. John gave himself time to explore his emotions instead of suppressing them, thus acknowledging disappointment. He went to his boss to get comments on why he wasn't chosen and to point out areas needing improvement. John signed up for a professional development course to hone his abilities and assumed extra responsibility to show leadership. He saw the setback as a brief diversion, thinking his efforts would pay off. John was praised for his tenacity and aggressive attitude within a year and promoted.

The larger influence of resilience

1. In Personal Development, Resilience helps you be confident and flexible, allowing you to seize chances more confidently.
2. In Relationships: Resilience helps you negotiate problems and assist loved ones in trying circumstances.

Employers reward strong people who can manage pressure, adapt to change, and solve problems in their line of work.

Resilience as a Constant Value

Regardless of the obstacles you encounter along the road, resilience is the link between your current position and your desired one. Developing this vital ability helps you negotiate uncertainty with optimism, bravery, and tenacity.

Resilience, therefore, is about conquering obstacles rather than avoiding them. Every challenge you overcome prepares you for the next, transforming hardship into an opportunity for growth.

Building Strength

One definition of resilience is the ability to persevere in adversity. It's about building the fortitude to confront and learn from challenges rather than avoiding them.

Develop a Solution-Oriented Viewpoint

Emphasizing solutions rather than issues can help you advance—even under difficult conditions.

- Ask, "What's one thing I can do to improve the situation?" instead of declaring, this is impossible.
- Encourage gratitude in yourself. Change your viewpoint by appreciating the positives—even in trying circumstances.

For instance, a solution-oriented individual assesses what went wrong, notes lessons learned and uses those ideas to guide their next project when one fails.

Standardize Obstacles

Accepting losses as inevitable in life diminishes their ability to trip you. Everyone has difficulties; resilient individuals' capacity to keep on distinguishes them.

- **Frame Failure:** See it as feedback rather than a reflection on your value.
- Ask yourself, after a setback, what did I learn? How may I keep becoming better?

For instance, a writer whose publishers reject their work utilizes the experience to improve it, securing a contract with a better publication.

Create effective coping strategies.

Though they provide momentary respite, ineffective coping mechanisms such as avoidance or overindulgence almost always solve the issue's underlying cause. Good coping skills foster long-term resilience.

- **Exercise produces endorphins that lower stress and raise mood.** One may make a big impact with running, yoga, or even a fast stroll.
- **Personal Interests in Creativity:** Pursues of creativity such as painting, writing, or music provide a means of emotional release.
- **Social Connection:** Talk to encouraging family members or friends to help you see things from another angle.

Develop Resilience and Emotional Control

1. Set a three-times-a-day timer for an emotional check-

in. Ask yourself when it goes off: What am I experiencing right now? Why am I experiencing this? This exercise increases awareness of emotions and mindfulness.

2. Resilience Journal: Write about one daily difficulty each evening. Note your handling of it, what you discovered, and what you may do differently the next time.

3. **Gratitude and Affirmations**: Start every morning by noting three things you are thankful for and then repeating a positive affirmation, like I am competent in managing whatever comes my way.

4. Resilience Role Models: Choose someone you respect for their tenacity. Consider how they could tackle a problem you are already working on and draw motivation from their approach.

The Story of Maya and Its Real-World Application Maya was shocked when her team failed to meet a crucial deadline at her fast-paced software firm due to unanticipated technological difficulties. As a result, Maya was subject to enormous pressure from above, while customers were unhappy and staff were demoralized.

Maya relied on her emotional regulation abilities to remain composed in the face of adversity rather than giving in to anger or placing blame. Maya paused to focus on her breathing, which helped to slow her rushing thoughts and emotions as part of her practice of emotional regulation. This allowed her to collect herself and tackle the issue logically instead of reacting emotionally. The team captain told herself she could choose how she would respond to the problems that were certain to arise. When she calmed down, Maya called a staff meeting to investigate the situation. Instead of wallowing in the project's failure, she said, we should be honest and transparent about where we went wrong.

They found that working together allowed room for development in many areas, including communication, testing, and preparing for unforeseen technological problems. Maya instituted weekly check-ins to track development and a system to evaluate risks to spot problems before they escalated.

She reassured her men by praising their resiliency and ability to overcome obstacles.

Maya was able to develop as a leader and use the setback as a learning opportunity because of her plan. Her colleagues and bosses respected her for keeping her cool under pressure, and she inspired and equipped her team to do great things.

The Synergy of Emotional Mastery and Resilience

Emotional mastery and resilience are interdependent qualities that, when developed, increase one's capacity to confront life's challenges boldly. They provide the mental and emotional tools for sticking with it when things go tough.

Emotional mastery fuels their interaction resilience.

You can keep yourself from being overwhelmed by setbacks and respond positively and productively if you control your emotions.

Keeping your cool under fire enables you to see a problem for what it is and figure out how to solve it.

Building Resilience Stimulates Mastery of Emotions

The ability to recover quickly from setbacks equips you with the mental fortitude to face the difficulties ahead gracefully.

As you overcome challenges, you gain self-assurance in your capacity to control your emotions.

Put this example into practice by considering what it might be like to apply for jobs and keep being turned down. Being emotionally competent helps you bounce back from setbacks without giving up. At the same time, resilience encourages you to refine your application materials, ask for critiques, and keep trying until you get your dream job.

Making Your Dream a Reality

Building resilience and emotional control requires a lifetime of practice. These abilities, when combined, provide the framework for a satisfying existence.

Applications of These Abilities

Reminding Oneself Every Day

Take some time out of your day to think about how you're feeling emotionally. Consider what happened to set off your emotions and your reaction to it. Emotional intelligence is improved using this method.

Practices That Build Resilience Journaling, activities to increase gratitude, and mindfulness meditation are all great ways to build resilience and get back up after a setback.

Reflect on What You learned from Every Setback. After a tough time, think about how you became stronger because of what you learned. You can now face future issues with more certainty thanks to this information.

Living a Life of Meaning and Contentment

You can better handle stress, failure, and uncertainty if you make emotional mastery and resilience a part of your everyday life. When you work on these abilities, you'll be able to face problems directly, keep your chin up, and believe in your potential for improvement and success.

By combining emotional maturity with resilience, you may accomplish your objectives and live a life of meaning and purpose, just as Maya did when she turned adversity into opportunity.

VICTOR IMHANS

SECTION SEVEN

CREATING FUTURE WORTHFUL RELATIONSHIPS

A good life is built upon relationships. Whether they are professional links to mentors and colleagues or personal ties to loved ones, the relationships you make greatly impact your emotional well-being, success, happiness, and experiences. Future masters of relationships must create links anchored in trust, empathy, and a common goal. It also requires developing resilience to negotiate challenges and remaining driven to foster and deepen these relationships over time. Meaningful relationships change, grow, and blossom with deliberate effort and attention—they are not fixed. Reliability in Interactions Every long-lasting relationship depends critically on resilience. It offers the means to negotiate conflicts, misinterpretation, or outside pressure without letting these difficulties sour ties. Rather, resilience helps relationships to flourish under hardship by encouraging mutual respect and understanding.

Important Elements of Relationship Resilience

1. **Handling Conflict Beautifully:** Any relationship will naturally involve conflict, which also offers chances for development. Approach conflicts with empathy and a readiness to grasp the other person's viewpoint instead of running from them.
2. For instance, stop to consider and gently communicate your emotions instead of reacting defensively in a fight with a friend. Speak from "I," saying things like, I am offended when... instead of assigning guilt.
3. **Accepting forgiveness or clinging to hatred or grudges strains relationships.** Forgiveness releases rather than about justifying destructive actions.

Emotional burdens and fostering healing for both parties.
4. **Developing Patience and Meaningful relationships takes time to grow and heal.** Patience lets you gently work through problems without rushing choices or generating pointless conflict.

Doable Advice for Developing Relationship Resilience

- **Self-Reflection:** Check your part in disagreements often. How may I help to bring about a solution?
- **Boundary Setting**: Clearly state your limits to guarantee mutual respect and help prevent misinterpretation.
- Stress Management: Practice stress-reduction techniques like deep breathing or mindfulness to remain calm and composed during disagreements.

The Foundation of Connection: Active Listening

Listening is about understanding emotions, validating experiences, and establishing a safe environment for honest communication—not just about hearing words. Stronger ties in both personal and professional life, as well as trust, are strengthened by active listening.

How to Use Active Listening

1. Put aside your phone, turn off alerts, and keep eye

contact to indicate real attention, eliminating distractions.
2. Validate Feelings Say something like, "I understand how that might make you feel, or That sounds challenging," to acknowledge the other person's feelings.
3. Ask open-ended inquiries such as, what do you think about...? or how did it make you feel? This will help to promote significant conversation.

For instance, a colleague complains about a project. Rather than swooping in with fixes, you pay close attention, probe clarifying questions, and validate their worries. This strategy develops cooperation and confidence.

Motivation in Social Interactions

Strong social ties provide a great reservoir of inspiration, responsibility, and drive. Surrounding driven, supportive people helps you to flourish both personally and professionally.

Techniques for Creating Inspired Relationships

Engage like-minded people. Look for those with your beliefs and goals. Participate in community activities, online forums, or professional networking groups.

Example: If you're passionate about fitness, joining a local running club or an online health community can provide encouragement and camaraderie.

Share Your Goals. Vocalizing your goals to trusted

individuals creates accountability. When others know what you're striving for, they can offer support, advice, and encouragement. Example: Share your intention to write a book with a close friend. They might check your progress, recommend resources, or join you in writing sessions.

Engage in Collaborative Growth or Collaborate on projects or efforts that connect with your interests. Working together creates mutual development and develops connections.

Example: Join a community garden effort with a buddy. The united effort and accomplishment will strengthen your connection and foster a sense of collective direction.

Building Relationships for Tomorrow

- Maintaining open lines of contact is especially important during busy times. Maintaining friendships can benefit much from a simple text, a phone call, or a handwritten letter.
- Give gratitude to those in your life. Small gestures of appreciation or praise strengthen relationships.
- Celebrate each other's accomplishments, whether reaching personal goals, getting promoted, or finishing a task.
- Celebrating with others fosters a sense of community and inspiration.
- Put in Time and Work Relationships require constant attention. Make time for your loved ones and participate in significant discussions or events.

Creating a Foundation for Supportive Network Illustration

Emma, a young entrepreneur, came to see she should surround herself with driven individuals. She met friends and mentors matching her desire when she joined a local business development club. Emma participated actively in group activities and discussed her goals, gaining important understanding and creating lifetime connections. These contacts gave him drive and responsibility, which enabled her to thrive.

Creating Close Relationships

Establishing deep, enduring relationships requires great work, sensitivity, and intention. Resilience support, targeted listening, and the creation of interesting connections assist relationships in overcoming obstacles and becoming stronger with time.

Remember that relationships demand ongoing maintenance and attention. Investing in your relationships will help you realize that the people in your life support, inspire, and improve your road to a happy, fulfilled future.

Apply in Real Life: Creating Support Systems

Maintaining resilience and driving calls for support systems.

For example, Sarah, a just-started business owner, began her company overwhelmed. She joined a club of nearby small business owners to share her challenges and get advice. This group kept her motivated and focused. Hence, it became her favorite source of direction and help finally.

Creating Your Support System

- Make the Most of Current Relationships Speak with friends, relatives, or coworkers who share your beliefs and objectives.
- **Widen Your Networks.** To meet new people, go to events, sign up for online groups, or take part in communities centered around hobbies.
- **Engage in Active Participation to Encourage and support others.** Reciprocity is the foundation of strong relationships.

Motivation and Resilience in Action

Future mastery of relationships calls for constant learning, emotional awareness, and goal orientation. Resilience, active listening, and surrounding yourself with inspiring people help you build a network of contacts that advances your welfare and personal development.

Your relationship effort now creates the framework for a future filled with deep partnerships and shared achievement. Let each touch be a step toward a life improved by trust, understanding, and cooperation.

VICTOR IMHANS

SECTION EIGHT

SHAPE A FUTURE ANCHORED ON HEALTH

Your life hinges primarily on your health. It enables you to overcome challenges, motivates you to reach targets, and raises your production. Without it, even the most fervent aspirations would seem unattainable.

In a health-first future, your physical and mental health are prioritized, laying the groundwork for long-term resilience, energy, and concentration.

You may improve the quality of your daily life and your ability to accomplish your objectives by consciously developing healthy relationships. This section explores the critical function resilience plays in preserving your health and offers doable tactics to remain inspired and attain long-term well-being.

Why Put Health First in the Future?

A health-first future involves more than simply being well or avoiding illness; it also entails realizing your full potential, developing resilience, and ensuring you can live life to the fullest and purposefully. Putting your well-being first today lays the groundwork for long-lasting vitality, mental clarity, and general contentment. Here's the reason this approach is very vital:

Energy and Concentration

Your health status drives your daily life. When nourished, active, and rested, your body provides the vitality to meet responsibilities, pursue your interests, and overcome challenges.

- **Physical Energy:** Maintaining a healthy lifestyle increases your physical energy, enabling you to be active and effective all day. Frequent exercise strengthens your muscles, improves circulation, and oxygenates your cells, allowing you to do hard activities with more endurance.
- **Mental Clarity:** Healthy eating and enough sleep promote cognitive function, which makes it possible to concentrate, think clearly, and solve issues efficiently. A healthy brain functions better, improving creativity, memory, and judgment.

For instance, picture beginning your day with a healthy breakfast, a vigorous stroll, and a restful night's sleep. Rather than grog from bad eating habits or lack of sleep, you will probably wake up feeling motivated, focused, and ready to meet difficulties.

Healing and Strength

Being healthy goes beyond avoiding problems; it also requires building the courage and adaptability to overcome emotional, physical, or psychological hurdles. Resilience helps you overcome obstacles and turn them into opportunities for personal growth.

- **Physical Resilience:** A strong, healthy body will recuperate from illnesses, stresses, and injuries more effectively. Frequent exercise boosts your immune system, and healthy eating and enough sleep give your body the tools to heal itself.
- **Mental and Emotional Resilience:** Emotional

health is bolstered by physical health. Exercise helps you control your anxiety and have a happy attitude by lowering stress hormones and releasing endorphins.

Example: A resilient person concentrates on physical rehabilitation, good habits, and keeping active in ways that accommodate their injury after suffering a minor injury during an exercise. This way of thinking keeps obstacles from ruining their road toward general well-being.

Lifespan and Life Quality

Making your health a priority now is an investment in the future. Living well is more important than just living longer. Maintaining your freedom, enjoying your achievements, and making a significant contribution to the world around you as you age are all made possible by having a health-first perspective.

- **Preventing Chronic Illness:** Good lifestyle choices lower the chance of developing long-term illnesses that might eventually lower quality of life, such as diabetes, arthritis, and heart disease.
- **Preserving Mobility and Independence:** Being strong and active guarantees that you may go on with your favorite activities, such as playing with your grandkids or traveling, without physical restrictions.
- **Improving Emotional Fulfillment:** You can fully participate in relationships, interests, and experiences when your body and mind are in good health, which enhances your life at every stage.

For instance, imagine yourself at 70, still hiking, volunteering, or engaging in your favorite pastimes because you put your health first in your early years. Your capacity to savor these times in the future is strongly impacted by the decisions you make now.

The Ripple Impact of Giving Health Top Priority

Giving your health a priority helps you and improves the people close to you. You are more suited to help your loved ones, be present at work, and encourage others to choose wellness when you are strong and healthy.

- **In Relationships:** Good health lets you be present and involved with friends and family, strengthening bonds.
- **In Your Career:** High energy and mental clarity boost output, creativity, and leadership, supporting professional greatness.
- **In Your Community:** Your health-first way of living encourages those around you to select healthier behaviors, creating a series of well-being.

The Role of Resilience in Medical Education

Maintaining and enhancing your health among the demands of life depends mostly on resilience. It is your capacity for adaptation, healing, and forward motion in adversity. Resilience helps you remain focused, make wise choices about your health, and maintain long-term wellness practices in an erratic environment, whether your path is one of disease, injury, or burnout.

Health resilience is about laying a foundation that will enable you to confidently and powerfully negotiate obstacles, not just about recovering. It helps you to see obstacles as chances for development, adaptation, and success.

Overcoming Setbacks

Setbacks like sickness, injury, or times of great stress may throw off your schedule and try your will. Resilience emphasizes what you can manage, gives the attitude and resources required to overcome these obstacles, and guides regular steps toward recovery.

- **Keep your positive attitude.** Although it's normal to be annoyed or demoralized after a setback, resilience lets you focus on ideas and forward rather than on constraints.
- **Make the best use of the resources at hand.** Medical specialists, physical therapists, or a support system of friends and family may all help in recovery. Resilience motivates you to search for and use these tools properly.

For instance, a biker suffering from a back ailment would first feel let down about being unable to exercise. Rather than giving up, they might remain active while letting their back heal by using the recuperation time to investigate other types of exercise, such as swimming, yoga, or upper-body strength activities.

Developing Physical Strength

Resilience is about developing strength and adaptability before problems start, not just rebounding back. Strong, healthy bodies are more suited to meet the demands of daily life, bounce back from hardship, and promote general well-being.

Frequent Workout

Resilience rests mostly on physical exercise. It improves flexibility and balance, strengthens your body, and boosts cardiovascular health, helping you readily meet physical obstacles.

Strength training increases muscle mass, corrects posture, and strengthens bones, lowering the chance of injuries.

- **Cardio Exercises:** Helps heart health and increases endurance, therefore arming your body to manage mental and physical stress.
- **Harmony and Flexibility; Balance Worksheets:** Yoga, Pilates, and tai chi improve mobility and help to lower the risk of strains or falls.

Balanced diet

A strong body depends on correct fuel. Whole foods abound in the nutrients required for healing, growth, and maintenance of best performance.

- **Emphasize nutrient-dense foods** with lean proteins, whole grains, fresh fruits, veggies, and healthy fats.

- **Stay Hydrated:** Appropriate amounts of water assist digestion, general body operation, and energy levels.
- **Support Healing and Immunity:** Crucially for immunological defense and recovery are nutrients such as vitamin C, zinc, and omega-3 fatty acids.

Recover and rest

resilience depends on your body and mind healing, replenishment, and readiness for the next day's demands.

- Try for seven to nine hours of nightly quality sleep to promote cognitive function, hormone balance, and muscular restoration.
- Incorporate active recovery—low-intensity exercises like walking or stretching on rest days—to increase circulation and lower stiffness.
- Learn techniques for relaxation. Progressive muscular relaxation, deep breathing, and meditation help to lower stress and improve recuperation.

The synergy of physical and mental resilience

Physical resilience is directly related to your mental and emotional health, not just your body. A strong body follows from a strong intellect and vice versa. Regular exercise, for instance, lowers tension and anxiety; mental resilience helps you remain motivated to maintain physical health routines even in an overwhelming life.

Practical Use: Real-life

When working as a professional, Sarah had persistent back pain;

she first felt annoyed by her restrictions. She utilized the challenge, however, to concentrate on low-impact workouts like swimming and included a nutrient-dense diet heavy in anti-inflammatory foods. She also worked on stress management using mindfulness meditation. Her physical suffering passed with time, and she came out stronger—physically and psychologically.

Techniques for Long-Term Wellness

Reaching and maintaining health requires a lifetime dedication to consistency, drive, and self-care rather than a one-time effort. When you use sensible, doable plans that keep you motivated and on target, wellness becomes ingrained in your life. Here's how to make long-term health realistic and gratifying:

Establish small objectives

Although big health objectives might seem overwhelming, they are more reachable and less frightening if broken into smaller, reasonable chunks. Small goals let you concentrate on quick, doable actions while gathering momentum toward more general goals.

- **Start small.** Set reasonable objectives, including shedding 5 pounds monthly or jogging for 10 minutes daily rather than trying to run a marathon or drop 50 pounds immediately.
- **Daily Routines Count:** Add tweaks that compound over time to your regimen. For instance, drink one additional glass of water every day, load your meals with more veggies and walk 2,000 more steps per day.

For instance, break up your ambitious goal—running a marathon—into smaller benchmarks: first finish a 5K, then a 10K, and so on. Every achievement fuels your confidence and keeps you head on.

Why It Works Little objectives make one successful. They provide regular victories that increase drive and help you stay involved and targeted, making the trip seem doable.

Track Your Development

Even if outcomes seem gradual, tracking your development shows how far you have come. It also guarantees that you keep on track by helping you see what is working and where changes may be required.

Instruments of Monitoring

- Log your exercises, food, water consumption, and sleep using apps like MyFitnessPal, Fitbit, or Strava.
- Real-time data on your activity level, heart rate, calories burned, and more accessible via smartwatches and fitness trackers.
- Journals: Note daily ideas, workouts, and meals in a digital notepad or document. Revealing patterns in your behavior might help you modify your health plan using journaling.

Track Unquantifiable Accomplishments

Not always measured by the scale or a stopwatch is progress. Celebrate little victories, including improved daily energy, better sleep and awakening, and more effective stress management.

For instance, someone monitoring their exercise program may find they can accomplish more repetitions or lift heavier weights even if their weight has not changed. This non-scale triumph shows actual development.

Why It Works: Whether numerical or sensory, seeing real-world outcomes supports good behavior and drives you. Even on difficult days, it gives purpose and a feeling of success.

Honor Turning Points

Maintaining drive requires an appreciation of your successes. Celebrations support good habits and make the road towards health fun and fulfilling.

How To Celebrate Wins

Praise yourself. When you mark a milestone, reward yourself with something.

- Unique, perhaps new clothes or exercise gear.
- Spa day or a restful massage.
- A favorite dinner or dessert devoid of guilt.

Involve other people: Tell encouraging friends, relatives, or a gym community about your development. Celebrating together builds shared pleasure and responsibility.

Establish Personal Habits: Create little ceremonies to

commemorate successes, such as drafting a congrats email, blogging about your development, or snapping a happy picture.

After a month of regular exercise, treat yourself to a night out with friends or a yoga class you have always wanted to try. Sharing your successes with others multiplies the happiness and motivates them to aim high.

Celebrating milestones allows you to relate positively to your job. This helps you keep your habits and be committed to your long-term health goals.

Including These Strategies into Your Daily Life

1. **Develop a well-defined plan.** List your long-term goal and break it up into more doable portions. Determine the everyday behaviors that will enable you to reach every milestone.
2. **Be consistent yet flexible:** Life might offer curveballs, so be ready to modify your strategy while being dedicated to your general goals.
3. **Stay Inspired:** Whether being active for your children, lowering your disease risk, or boosting your body confidence, routinely review your "why."

Practical Use Case

Forty-year-old professional John wants to increase his fitness and shed pounds. He began by pledging 15 minutes daily for walking, then progressively worked for 45 minutes over three months. Using a fitness app, he recorded his steps and honored achievements by treating himself to better forms of his favorite foods. John dropped twenty pounds, had more energy, and developed long-term sustainable practices using these techniques.

Constructing a Sustainable Healthy Life

Establishing a health-first future is about ingraining wellness into your everyday life so that it comes naturally, not about transient solutions or routines. Even with the pressures of life and uncertainty, a sustainable, health-first lifestyle guarantees that your physical and mental well-being remains a top priority. Here's how to do this:

1. Make nonnegotiable health nonnegotiable

It is not an optional chore; health should be given first attention. Making health-related activities—such as exercise, food planning, and rest—nonnegotiable guarantees they become second nature in your schedule.

How to apply this?

- **Block time for wellness.** Plan as you would for crucial meetings or deadlines: schedule exercises, smart food preparation, and leisure time. Approach these visits with the same degree of dedication.
- **Consistency Over Perfection:** To strengthen the habit, schedule little activities, including a 10-minute walk or a fast, nutrient-dense snack, even on hectic days.

For instance, a working professional, Sarah, plans her Monday exercises for 6:30 a.m. She creates consistency—even on busy days—by seeing this time as holy and nonnegotiable.

2. Determine Your "Why."

Many times, motivation arises from a more profound goal. Knowing why health counts to you personally can help you stay dedicated to your wellness path, even in the face of obstacles.

Think back on your goal:

- **Family & Loved Ones:** Keeping fit and healthy can help you to spend time with your spouse, grandkids, or children.
- **Disease Prevention:** Lowering the risk of obesity, heart disease, or diabetes among other chronic conditions
- **Self-improvement:** reaching personal objectives, building confidence, or improving your quality of living.

John's "why," for instance, is his children. He wants to keep active, so he may offer a good example of a healthy lifestyle by playing soccer with them. This helps him stay driven and prioritize his health, even on demanding days.

3. Create a System of Support

One does not have to start a health-first lifestyle by itself. Your possibilities of achievement will be substantially raised by surrounding yourself with encouraging people who share or support your objectives.

Strategies for Developing Support:

- Join a community: Take advantage of wellness organizations, online forums, or exercise courses where like-minded people exchange ideas and support.
- Share your aspirations with friends or family and encourage them to accompany you. Including others generates responsibility and shared inspiration, whether for a weekly stroll or a shared healthy dinner.
- Ask a personal trainer, dietician, or health coach for professional guidance and structure to fit your program.

For instance, Maria joined a nearby jogging club to increase her fitness level. Her motivation was sustained by the companionship, camaraderie, and reciprocal support, which also formed new friendships.

4. remain adaptable

Rigid plans may easily break apart in life when unanticipated occurrences develop. Being flexible helps you adjust without losing sight of your main health objectives.

Adjusting to Difficulties:

- **Change Your Approach:** If you miss the gym, try a little bodyweight exercise at home. If meal planning is not feasible one week, choose quick, reasonably priced choices from your grocery shop.

- **Pay more attention to development than perfection.** Know that the road has obstacles. Resilience enables your recovery and future motion.
- **Have backup plans,** such as fast workouts or easy-to-make meals, to keep on target in hectic or trying circumstances.

For instance, Mark changed from hour-long gym sessions to 20-minute high-intensity interval training (HIIT) at home when his work calendar became more demanding. This adaptability maintained his exercise schedule even under time restrictions.

Maintaining Your First Lifestyle: Health

Think about these extra ideas to make health a constant in your life:

Accept Habit Stacking

Match fresh health behaviors with current routines. For instance, make a nutritious meal while preparing morning coffee or stretch while watching TV.

Consistently Review Objective

Your priorities in health change as life does. Review your objectives sometimes and change them to fit your present situation and ambitions.

Honor Your Path Forward

Acknowledge and value your development. Even little

successes support good conduct and help you to be successful generally.

The Health-First Perspective

A health-first approach to life is not a band-aid solution but a transient patch. It's about learning to be resilient, promising to be constantly consistent, and appreciating the trip instead of striving for perfection. It's the knowledge that little, persistent, intentional deeds might have a great, long-lasting effect.

This kind of thinking will help you prioritize your well-being in a significant and sustainable manner, laying the foundation for a full, powerful, and vivid life.

1. Consistency's predominance over excellence

Consistency over perfection is one of the major principles of the health-first frame of perspective. Perfection may be undulating and unreachable, causing fatigue and dissatisfaction. Conversely, regular, little acts are doable, create momentum, and result in lifelong habits.

- **The Reasons It Works:** Though little daily activities like eating a nutritious snack, jogging for ten minutes, or drinking an additional glass of water appear, over time, they add up to notable improvement.
- **For instance**, start with 15 minutes of daily activity and progressively expand as you develop stamina and confidence instead of immediately attempting to follow a rigorous training plan.

Learn to value improvement rather than perfection. Every action, no matter how tiny, advances your health objectives.

2. Valuing Resilience

Resilience is the capacity to change, bounce back, and remain ahead of obstacles. A health-first approach recognizes that the road includes setbacks—from missed workouts to bad meals to moments of stress. Resilience helps you perceive these events as chances to reset and flourish rather than failures.

Resilience Building Techniques:

- **Learn from failures.** Reflect on the difficulty and how you could change going forward.
- **Develop self-compassion:** Treat yourself kindly; understand that perfection is neither required nor realistic.
- **Remain flexible:** Be ready to change your strategies should life curveballs arise.

For instance, Sarah, a working teacher, chose shorter, more easily available exercises like stretching or walking instead of skipping entirely when she missed her planned workouts during a particularly trying week. Her agility kept her on target and avoided shame or despondency.

Resilience, therefore, is about remaining committed and rebounding back even on a non-linear road.

3. Discovering Pleasure in the Approach

Wellness should be a cause of delight and pleasure, not a duty. A health-first perspective helps you support your well-being through activities and behaviors that offer you satisfaction.

- **Make It Pleasurable:** Look for activities, foods, and habits you like. This may be yoga outside, dancing, or creating colorful dishes.
- **Celebrate Small Wins:** Honor and treat yourself for any improvement, no matter how small it appears. Acknowledging successes keeps you involved and driven.
- **Pay close attention to positivism.** Change your perspective from "I have to" to "I get to." Say, for example, "I get to move my body and feel stronger" rather than "I have to work out."

For instance, John found group exercise programs were more fun than alone gym visits. The group's friendship and enthusiasm kept him driven, transforming exercise from a chore into a joy of his week.

The lesson is that fitness becomes a fulfilling and lasting part of your life when it fits your hobbies and passions.

4. Little Actions, Great Influence

The health-first perspective stresses the need for little, daily efforts. Though initially small, these micro choices have a domino effect that changes your lifestyle and health over time.

- One little action may be rising each morning and drinking a glass of water.
- Changing one daily processed snack for a whole food choice.
- I'm Having a five-minute mindfulness break right now at work.
- Choosing to walk to a neighboring retailer rather than drive.

The Reasons It Works: These little deeds are doable, repetitious, and progressively form into more natural and durable habits.

The lesson is not to undervalue the power of little actions as they form the basis of long-lasting transformation.

5. Saving for Your Future

Giving your health priority is investing in your future self. A health-first approach guarantees the physical vitality, mental clarity, and emotional resilience to celebrate your successes and significantly improve your relationships and community.

- Long-term benefits include lower risk of chronic conditions.
- As you become older, you have more freedom and movement.
- Improved quality of life, full of energy and goal orientation.

For instance, 50-year-old businesswoman Lisa started paying more attention to her health by making small adjustments like walking after meals and including more vegetables. She discovered a year later that she was more vivacious, motivated, and suited to meet her family's and work pressures.

The lesson is that every effort you make now prepares the path for a better, more contented future.

VICTOR IMHANS

SECTION NINE

FOCUSING ON A FUTURE-BASED CAREER

Given the economic and technical advancements in a world that is quickly changing, a job with a future orientation is essential. Starting such a job calls for tenaciousness to overcome obstacles, flexibility to welcome change, and a great will to reach long-term objectives.

Developing Professional Resilience

Professional resilience is the ability to soar above challenges, adapt to field circumstances, and bloom under duress. Clear-cut professions are rare; most provide chances for growth, change, and uncertain periods. Developing resilience ensures that you remain calm and proactive even in the face of unforeseen obstacles.

Adapting with Industrial Trends

Today's industries are changing at a rate never seen before. Technologies like automation and artificial intelligence are redefining roles, so professionals must remain knowledgeable and flexible. An example would be a software engineer who learns contemporary programming languages like Python or JavaScript to maintain outdated systems. This assures their relevance in the future and offers access to innovative ideas such as artificial intelligence and blockchain development.

Succeeding in front of failure

missed promotions, project failures, or layoffs test your perseverance. Resilient employees perceive setbacks as opportunities for introspection, development, and course correction rather than being causes of obsession.

After a layoff, for instance, a marketing specialist investigates freelancing and gains a range of knowledge before starting a profitable consultancy.

Maintaining Opportunity and Risk Control

Resilience is shown by your capacity to take reasonable risks—that is, by looking for new jobs or fields that complement your objectives.

Methods for Building Professional Resilience

- **Continuous Learning:** To stay competitive, upgrade your skill set regularly. Take classes, attend seminars, or look into credentials pertinent to your work.
- **Accept Change:** Consider changes in the sector as chances for development rather than dangers.
- **Self-care:** Preserve your physical and mental health so you can face the demands of your job with vigor and clarity.

Maintaining Motivation for Professional Growth

Success in the workplace is fueled by motivation. Long-term professional excitement, however, requires strategic planning and intentional work.

Describe Your Why

- A distinct sense of purpose fuels long-term motivation.

Consider why your profession is important and how it fits your long-term goals.

Sample Questions: How do I want to influence my field?

- How does my job help me achieve my objectives, such as work-life balance or financial independence?

Exercise: Summarize your beliefs and professional aspirations in a career mission statement. Regularly review this statement to help you remember your "why."

Request Input

One of the most important tools for development is constructive criticism. Seeking feedback from mentors, coworkers, or superiors regularly aids in skill development and helps you remain on course.

How to Make the Most of Feedback

- Keep an open mind and concentrate on progress rather than criticism when you get comments.
- Create a strategy of action to handle the areas the comments point up for development.

Strategic Networking

Professional networks provide opportunities, drive, and support. Spend time around others who inspire and challenge you to grow.

Establishing a strong network requires:

- Attending industry events, webinars, and conferences and meeting professionals aligned with your interests.
- Participate in forums or online communities related to your profession.
- Develop connections by providing them with something of value, like resources or ideas.

Example in Action: a graphic designer, Maria, joined a local design meeting group after feeling her job was stagnating. She connected with seasoned experts there who provided guidance and insights into new trends. Maria got a job at a prestigious creative firm after updating her portfolio in less than a year.

Putting Your Career in the Future

Adaptability and a dedication to development are the cornerstones of future-oriented employment. You may succeed in any professional setting by coordinating your activities with your long-term goals and being adaptable to change.

Future-Proofing Advice

1. **Determine New Trends:** Keep abreast of changes in your industry and technological breakthroughs.
2. **Develop Transferable Skills:** Gain industry-translatable soft skills, including critical thinking, communication, and leadership.
3. **Review a range of prospects:** Look for jobs in remote work environments, freelancing, and startups, not limited to traditional career paths.

Resilience and drive are essential abilities rather than qualities one may develop over time. Developing these qualities will help you create a future-oriented career that complements your values and objectives.

SECTION TEN

NURTURING CREATIVITY AND INNOVATION

Creativity and invention are the engines that accelerate progress, resolve difficulties, and accomplish personal happiness. Both of these engines are essential to the success of these endeavors. Whether you are an artist, an entrepreneur, or a professional, cultivating your creativity may help you break through barriers, find new ideas, and bring value to your life and career. This is true regardless of whether you are a professional, an entrepreneur, or an artist. Conversely, the path to creativity is not always a strigose; it usually calls for overcoming obstacles, negotiating moments of uncertainty, and surviving periods of stagnation while one is on the road to invention. Regarding developing creative potential, one must combine resilient and creative traits with the will to keep the spark alive. It is necessary to do this to maintain the spark.

Both ingenuity and perseverance are important aspects of this.

The creative process is not complete without trial and error. For every brilliant idea that ultimately succeeds, there may be infinite unsuccessful attempts. Failure is not a point of no return when you have resilience; rather, it is a stepping stone to progress. When you have resilience, you can perceive failure with this perspective.

1. Recognizing the Significance of the Role That Failure Contributes

Every step of the creative process is fundamentally loaded with the prospect of failure. You can increase your strength, better your plan, and evaluate your preconceptions with every hurdle you face.

Example: Before Harry Potter became one of the most beloved book series of all time, the manuscript that J.K. Rowling had written the Harry Potter series was rejected by twelve different publishers around the globe. Publishers. Her perseverance was aided by her resiliency and her trust in her mission.

2. Embracing the Iterative Process

The creative process is seldom linear. Oftentimes, one must go back to concepts, rework ideas, and start the process all over again. Being strong helps you to concentrate on the overall objective, even in cases where the immediate results fall short of your expectations.

Here are some practical guidelines to help creative endeavors be resilient:

- **See failure from another angle:** rather than declaring, "I failed," you may remark, "I learned what doesn't work."
- Honor modest accomplishments include completing a rough draft, picking up a new skill, or getting helpful criticism. Celebrate your successes and treat yourself for moving forward.
- You should seek support by discussing your creative challenges with peers or mentors who may provide you with encouragement and a different point of view.

Keeping Oneself Motivated via Creative Activities

It is the fuel that supports creativity, particularly during times of uncertainty or stagnation, and motivation fulfills this function. You can make constant progress if you implement techniques that will maintain your creative energy at a high level.

Take part in free-form play

Creative endeavors flourish in settings devoid of criticism. Experiment with different concepts, materials, or processes to have fun without concern about the results.

For instance, a painter can go outside their typical style and produce abstract pieces to experiment with new methods and rekindle their enthusiasm for their craft.

To engage in playful exploration, it is recommended to set aside a certain amount of weekly time for "unstructured creativity," where the primary objective is to enjoy the process.

If you are a writer, you should try sculpting; if you are a musician, you should try dancing. Both of these activities are radically different from your typical profession.

Collaborate

Working together may be a fertile ground for creative expression. When you collaborate with other people, you have access to new ideas, views, and energy that you can share.

Exemplification: Two businesspeople who possess talents that are complimentary to one another, one of whom focuses on technical competence and the other on marketing, combine their strengths to develop a unique product.

Participate in creative groups, whether locally or online, to establish connections with persons with similar interests and values.

By working together on minor tasks, you may ascertain whether or not you are compatible with one another and investigate the possibility of merging your efforts.

Setting clear goals and communicating honestly are two of the most important things that can be done to ensure alignment and mutual respect.

Set Challenges

If you want to break through creative barriers and come up with new ideas, setting challenges for yourself might be of assistance to you. These difficulties provide structure and a feeling of achievement, which fuels drive; they create structure.

An example would be a writer who commits to writing one short story every week for one month, while a designer may set a goal to finish a daily sketching assignment.

One way to create effective challenges is to make them time-bound, like a project lasting thirty days or a goal set every week.

You should choose projects that challenge your capabilities without causing you to feel overwhelmed.

Ensure you communicate your progress to others to maintain accountability and get feedback.

Instruments that are Useful for Creative and Innovative Thinking

Mind Mapping Tools, Number One

You may use applications such as Mind Meister or Miro to arrange thoughts and graphically investigate the relationships between different notions.

An example would be a graphic designer using a mind map to explore different themes, colors, and design components while developing ideas for a client's possible brand identity.

Keeping an Idea Journal

Maintain a specialized notebook or a digital application (such as Evernote) to record ideas as they occur to you.

Make it a habit to regularly analyze and elaborate on your notes to transform ideas into plans that can be implemented.

Creative Workspaces

Designing a physical or digital location that encourages creative thinking is the third step in the creative workspace process. Ensure Please, provide information, pictures, and tools that might trigger ideas.

For instance, an artist would set up their studio so that supplies such as paints, canvases, and reference materials are easily accessible. This will create an atmosphere that stimulates the artist to make on the spot.

Taking up Creative Challenge

During her creative process, Lisa, a graphic designer, had a sense of unease. She committed to making one poster per day for the duration of the thirty-day design challenge that she started. The posters would be based on random suggestions. She was able to explore new trends, improve her abilities, and rekindle her enthusiasm for design by the time the month came to a close.

How You Can Put This into Practice:

- Select a media or skill you want to improve upon.
- Set an attainable goal, such as completing one modest project per day.
- To ensure you are held responsible, share your progress with your peers or online.

Creativity and innovation in common place activities

Being an artist or an inventor is unnecessary to get the benefits of creativity. Through applying creative thinking to problem-solving, relationships, and difficulties in the workplace, it is possible to open doors you could not have expected.

Creativity in Everyday Life

- Perform the exercise known as "What If?" Asking yourself, "What if I approached this from a completely different perspective?" is a thought-provoking activity you might do when facing a dilemma.
- Gain Knowledge from Other Domains: Investigate fields that are not connected to your own to obtain ideas and inspiration.
- Maintain your natural curiosity by setting a goal to acquire new knowledge regularly. This might be a new skill, a recipe, or a piece of history.

Where Resilience and Creativity Intersect

Resilience and creativity are quite closely entwined. You grow more ready to take chances and explore and become more resilient. Likewise, creative inquiry teaches you to see obstacles as opportunities for development, enhancing resilience. All taken together, they enable you to be innovative, flexible, and successful in all spheres of life.

You release the ability to invent, solve issues, and realize your ideas by developing your creativity and matching it with resilience. Whether your goals are personal or professional, resilience and creativity are great tools for laying a successful and fulfilled future.

SECTION ELEVEN

FINANCIAL MASTERY FOR THE FUTURE

For one to have a rich and fulfilling future, it is vital to have complete control over their financial status. This gives you the liberty to pursue the things that are passionate about you, the resilience to deal with the unpredictability of life, and the capacity to leave behind a legacy that is significant to you when you die. In the current economic environment, which is always shifting, achieving financial resilience and maintaining the motivation to generate money is necessary. In this part, we will look into practical techniques and attitudes that can assist you in taking charge of your financial future.

Financial Planning

Setbacks in terms of finances are unavoidable. It is possible for even the most well-prepared plans to be put to the test by market downturns, unforeseen medical bills, or abrupt job loss. When it comes to planning your finances, having resilience implies that you will be able to recover from these challenges with self-assurance and consistency.

Unexpected Events and Their Implications

It is possible to conceive of an emergency fund as a financial safety net that protects you from sudden and unexpected expense disturbances in your financial situation. Save enough money to cover your living costs for at least three to six months.

An illustration of this would be how Lisa avoided taking on high-interest debt since her emergency fund was enough to pay the cost of repairs when her automobile suddenly broke down.

How to Establish a Fund for Unexpected Events

Begin with a tiny amount: contribute from each paycheck, even if it's just twenty dollars each week.

You should use automated transfers to automate your savings and guarantee that regular contributions are made.

Building up an emergency fund is a process that takes some time, but consistent progress builds up over time. This is why consistency is more important than speed.

Developing a financial contingency plan and diversifying revenue sources to lessen dependency on a single income source are also steps.

In the employment market, keeping a competitive advantage by keeping your résumé and skill set up to date is important.

Many different types of insurance should be considered when minimizing potential financial risks. Some examples of these types of insurance are health insurance, disability insurance, and renter's insurance. A strong sense of purpose, tenacity, and strategy are all necessary components of the drive to increase one's wealth. Keeping yourself motivated is needed to maintain the discipline required to accomplish your financial objectives.

Imagine being financially independent.

Imagine the advantages of having financial stability, such as retiring earlier, touring the globe, providing for your children's education, or beginning a project you are passionate about.

Exercise in Constructing Images: While you close your eyes, see the future you want to have. In your opinion, what does it look like to be financially independent? Put this vision down on paper so that you may utilize it as a source of inspiration.

Get Yourself Educated

Finance literacy gives you the ability to make choices based on accurate information.

Books like as "Books such as "Rich Dad Poor Dad" by Robert Kiyosaki and Benjamin Graham's "The Intelligent Investor" are both examples of such books. Examples of resources that need to be investigated.

Coursera, Khan Academy, and Udemy are examples of online platforms that provide courses or platforms.

Podcasts that provide a comprehensive breakdown of investing techniques and personalized financial advice.

Steps that may be taken to maintain engagement include devoting 15–30 minutes daily to studying financial matters.

The best way to remain up to speed on the latest trends is to join financial literacy clubs or attend webinars.

Establish Milestones: breaking down one's financial objectives into more manageable sections makes them more attainable and less intimidating.

One example of a financial milestone is that you will save $1,000 for an emergency fund in three months. You will pay off the bill with one credit card for six months.

Raise the amount of money contributed to retirement funds by 2% annually.

When you cross a major mark, treat yourself to keep your high degree of inspiration. If you have set aside a certain sum for dinner at your preferred restaurant, you should indulge yourself with a little delight.

Financial Growth Strategies

1. Creating a Successful Budget

- Create a zero-based budget wherein every dollar is assigned a defined use.
- To keep track of your income and spending, you should use budgeting applications such as Mint, YNAB (You Need A Budget), or Every Dollar.

2. Investe with Purposeful Intention

- To take advantage of compound interest, you should begin investing early.
- Including stocks, bonds, and real estate helps you to vary your portfolio and lower your risk load.
- Look at ways to invest ethically in line with your values, including green energy funds or social impact projects.

3. Clearing Debt First

- Focus on clearing debt with high interest rates—debt from credit cards.

When dealing with several debts, you may use the snowball technique, which involves beginning with the lowest sums, or the avalanche method, which starts with the highest interest rates.

The Transformation of Financial Habits: An Example from Real Life

A marketing manager, Michael battled to make ends meet from payday to paycheck. He began by putting aside fifty dollars from each paycheck to establish an emergency fund. In addition to that, he participated in an online personal finance course, which assisted him in gaining a better understanding of budgeting and investing. Michael could pay off $15,000 in debt over two years, establish a retirement fund, and now make a monthly contribution of $500 to his savings account.

Important Lessons to Learn for Financial Mastery

- To achieve stability, it is necessary to have financial resilience. Create a reserve for unexpected expenses and diversify your sources of income.
- Strong motivators include well-articulated objectives, a commitment to lifelong learning, and the ability to appreciate successes.

- Building wealth calls for time. Stay dedicated, adjust to circumstances, and keep a close eye on your goal—financial freedom.

You give yourself the ability to face the future with self-assurance, independence, and a sense of purpose when you take control of your financial situation. Today is the day to take the first step, and you will see a huge change in your financial life.

VICTOR IMHANS

SECTION TWELVE

THE SPIRITUAL DIMENSIONS

Spirituality bridges the gap between your inner world and the outside factors shaping your life. It provides resilience, clarity, strength, direction, and meaning in peaceful and trying circumstances. By fostering trust in a higher power, a connection to nature, or a practice of personal introspection, spirituality may help you manage your destiny, promoting balance, motivation, and great satisfaction.

Resilience Using Spiritual Techniques

One very effective instrument for developing resilience is spirituality. Particularly during life's most challenging times, it provides a feeling of optimism, grounding, and perspective. Connecting to something greater than yourself helps you to develop the emotional and mental fortitude needed to meet challenges.

Developing Spiritual Resilience

1. Pray.

- Offers solace and link to your inner self or a higher power.
- Offers times for reflection, gratitude, and the opportunity to seek guidance in tough situations.

After a job loss, for example, Mark found peace and comfort in prayer, which helped him to remain positive and focused.

2. Meditate

- Encouragement of living in the now allows one to acquire emotional balance and awareness.

- Regular meditation helps one approach problems with clarity and composure, therefore separating from stresses.

For instance, Sarah committed ten minutes daily to a guided meditation as she was overburdened with household duties. She felt more focused and suited over time to manage her hectic calendar.

3. Reflect

- Reflecting on previous events—through journaling or contemplation—helps you process emotions, gain understanding, and evolve.
- Acknowledging trends of strength and areas needing work increases self-awareness.

Maria, for instance, turned to writing for comfort after losing a loved one. She came to see her inner power and the lessons her experiences had imparted via thought.

Drive from a Greater Goal

Linking your activities to a greater goal helps regular work to become meaningful endeavors. Whether motivated by spiritual convictions, personal ideals, or a need to support the greater good, matching your objectives with a higher purpose produces long-lasting inspiration.

Strategies for Recognizing and Linking with Your Higher Purpose

1. Think about your opinions.

- Think about the morals and ideas that guide your life.
- To probe issues like: What counts to me? Legacy, I want to leave behind?

2. Contribute to a Greater Good

- Whether by volunteering, mentoring, or campaigning for issues close to your values, help to contribute to a Greater Good.
- John, a teacher, sees his work as a vocation to help mold the next generations. This viewpoint allows him to remain dedicated even in demanding academic years.

3. Search for meaning in daily activities.

- When related to your goal, even little chores may have great importance.
- For instance, a baker who views their creations as bringing happiness via food gets satisfaction in every bread they produce.

Why It Works: Your motivation to keep knowing that your activities help contribute to something significant comes from your efforts aligning with a greater goal.

Including spirituality in regular life

Spirituality may fit your daily schedule without regard to certain practices or venues. Little, deliberate actions support your being grounded, aligned, and linked to your ideals.

1. Early Customs

Beginning your day with intention:

- **Gratitude:** Remember three things you are glad to foster optimism.
- Spend five to ten minutes meditating or practicing deep breathing to create a calm, concentrated tone.
- **Statements of affirmation:** Say affirmations that fit your objectives, like "I am strong, purposeful, and capable."

2. Match Values with Behavior

Review your decisions often to make sure they represent your values and goals.

- For instance, should compassion be fundamental in seeking everyday chances to show compassion—such as supporting a colleague or neighbor?

3. Exercise conscious presence.

Whether working, hanging out with friends, or unwinding, be present in your actions. This awareness lowers stress and strengthens your relationship to the present.

4. Create a Spiritual Gathering

Talk to people you share in spiritual or moral compass.

- Go to church, join a mindfulness or meditation group, or help a cause consistent with your beliefs.

For instance, Emily, an entrepreneur, began helping at a food bank after joining a nearby meditation group. These ties enabled her to manage her rigorous career and gave her more direction.

Applied Real-Life: Emily's Change

Successful businesswoman Emily discovered she felt alienated even with her success. Looking for balance and clarity, she included little spiritual activities into her regimen:

Emily started every morning with three things she appreciated, which changed her viewpoint and raised her attitude.

She started a meditation group and volunteered every Saturday at a nearby food bank. These pursuits brought her back a feeling of direction.

Emily worked on being present at meetings and family meals, enhancing her connections and concentration.

Results: Emily rediscovered her beliefs and got the fresh drive to achieve personally and professionally by including spirituality in her everyday life.

The transforming influence of spirituality

Spirituality is a deep instrument for human development, self-discovery, and fulfillment—not just a habit. It provides a prism through which you can see life's difficulties as chances for personal development. Even under trying circumstances, spirituality offers clarity, resilience, and a deeper sense of purpose by helping one to connect to one's inner self and something higher.

Turning Obstacles into Possibilities for Personal Growth

Obstacles abound in life that test your character and will. Spirituality helps you face these difficulties with kindness and inquiry, enabling them to become drivers of personal development.

- **Reframing Struggles:** Spirituality helps you perceive challenges as lessons or stepping stones toward a better, more resilient self instead of as losses.
- **Getting Perspective:** Spirituality may help you see events more generally using introspection or prayer, therefore separating from present concerns. Usually, this change exposes latent abilities or answers.
- **Spiritual activities** such as writing, meditation, or interacting with a spiritual group help foster inner growth. Greater awareness of your emotions, ideals, and aspirations follows from this self-consciousness.

For instance, Sarah resorted to meditation and writing after a job loss to help her sort through her feelings and choose her next direction. Using these techniques, she discovered her love for instruction and started down a fresh, professional path that would provide happiness and contentment.

Anchoring Yourself in Uncertain Times

Though uncertainty might be uncomfortable, spirituality

provides a basis for consistency. It reminds you that you belong to something more and links you to a feeling of optimism and direction.

- Practices like mindfulness or prayer help you find comfort and basis in hard situations, allowing you to tackle uncertainty with a calm, open mind.
- Whether rooted in religious beliefs or personal philosophy, faith gives optimism that you have the inner ability to overcome challenges.
- **Encouragement of Trust:** Spirituality frequently stresses letting go of control and accepting that events follow their natural course and that every experience has value.

James, for instance, found comfort in daily thanks during a moment of financial instability. Considering the benefits he still had—family, health, and encouraging friends—helped him keep optimism and move deliberately toward financial security.

Bringing Actions with a Greater Goal

Spirituality helps you to relate your everyday behavior with your long-term goals and basic beliefs. This connection produces a life of aim, meaning, and satisfaction.

1. **Living Authentically**: Reflecting on your spiritual convictions can help you ensure your choices align with what is important to you, promoting integrity and peace.
2. **Finding Meaning in Daily Life:** They become meaningful when one links their regular chores to a

greater good. For example, cooking a dinner for your family becomes a loving and serving deed.
3. Many spiritual traditions stress compassion and service, which motivates you to help to improve the world.

For instance, Emily, a small company owner, sees her efforts as more than just a means of revenue. She sees them as a chance to help her neighborhood by offering mentoring and high-quality goods to aspirational businesses. This viewpoint drives her enthusiasm and helps her stay close to her goal.

Including spirituality in your daily regimen

Reaping the rewards of spirituality requires flexibility, not a strict framework. The secret is choosing activities that appeal to you and fit naturally into your life.

Concepts for daily spiritual activities:

1. Starting your day with thanks can help you to create goals consistent with your spiritual ideals.
2. Set aside five to ten minutes for conscious breaks like prayer, silent meditation, or deep breathing during your day.
3. Remember your day, noting times of connection, thankfulness, and personal development.
4. Volunteer, mentor, or participate in acts of compassion reflecting your spiritual views.

Your Peace and Purpose

Spirituality is like a lighthouse that leads you confidently and clearly through the complexity of life. Including spiritual practices in your life helps you develop inner calm, a feeling of direction in your activities, and a sense of great significance in your path.

- **Peace:** Grounding techniques help you grow the inner calm required to meet obstacles with serenity.
- **Purpose**: Spirituality helps you link your activities and aims to a greater purpose through intention.
- **Meaning:** Spirituality guides you toward value and delight in daily life, whether by connection, service, or introspection.

As you negotiate life's possibilities and difficulties, let your spiritual dimension serve as a compass. Investigate activities that speak to you and include them in your daily schedule. Thanks to the transforming force of spirituality, you will find a life that is strong and satisfying.

FINAL THOUGHTS YOUR STRAIGHT ROAD

There are three ways to become indestructible: self-discovery, perseverance, and lifelong learning. It is not about aiming for perfection or avoiding life's responsibilities but about strengthening the will to face challenges head-on and use tragedy as an opportunity for growth. To be indestructible is to have a mentality, body, and existence that can resist daily life's challenges and flourish.

Although this road is not straight and not always simple, it is fulfilling. Every challenge you face, every barrier you get past, every stride forward is evidence of your will and your determination to be the greatest version of yourself.

Main Takeaways

1. Resilience: An Ability You Acquire

You develop resilience by experience, practice, and tenacity; it is not something you are born with. Embracing obstacles and learning from them helps you to become stronger and more competent in managing the next problems.

2. The Value of Alignment

Mastery your mind, body, and life are about finding harmony and alignment. Working together harmoniously, these components release your potential and lead to a meaningful, deliberate life.

3. Your Travel Is Different

The road to becoming indestructible is not one-size-fits-all.

Your path is specifically yours, molded by your circumstances, ideals, and aspirations. Celebrate your uniqueness and respect the development you bring about throughout.

4. Encourage Others with Your Power

As you change your own life, others are motivated to follow suit. Your tenacity, will, and success become a lighthouse of hope for people around you, showing that everyone can develop and change.

Get Unbreakable

Being indestructible is about accepting life as it is, the pleasures, the challenges, and everything in between. It's about realizing that every difficulty you encounter is a chance for you to develop stronger and that pain frequently results from change.

- **Get stronger.** See failures as teachings when you run into them. "What can I learn from this?" you ask yourself, then utilize those realizations to advance.
- **Recognize Your Development:** There is no step small enough to honor. No matter how little it appears, every accomplishment lays a brick toward a stronger and more confident you.

Dedicated to lifelong development: The road to becoming indestructible changes rather than ends. Keep defining objectives, learning, and challenging yourself to reach fresh benchmarks.

Your Trip Starts Now

The moment you dedicate yourself to your development marks the start of your road toward an unbroken existence. It's about beginning where you are, with what you have, and moving consistently forward—not about waiting for the ideal moment or perfect circumstances.

Practical Advice for Starting Your Trip

1. **Consider Your Objectives.** To you, what does an unbroken existence look like? List your goals and outline your way to reach them.
2. **Beginning small is important.** Whether adopting a gratitude practice, starting an exercise program, or establishing clear limits, name one habit or attitude change you focus on right now.
3. **Accept the Procedure Know that the road involves difficulties.** What counts is your capacity for ongoing forward motion.

An infinitely potential life

You have the ability within you to mold your fate and lead a life that best represents your utmost potential. Your will to develop from obstacles defines your strength beyond your capacity to face them.

- **Unwavering Determination:** Though the road seems challenging, remain dedicated to your objectives. You know that every effort you make is moving you toward your goal.

- **Motivational Others:** Your path is evidence of what everyone is capable of, not just yours. Tell your experience and motivate others to start their road toward resilience and personal development.

Your Perfect Life to Come

We should start right now. Enter your indestructible existence with confidence, bravery, and a heart open. Let your deeds now provide the groundwork for a life full of meaning, fortitude, and satisfaction.

Recall that the road toward an indestructible existence is one of development rather than perfection. Every little advance marks a success. You possess the ability, the will, and the strength to design the life you have always imagined.

Your unbroken path starts today. Accept it and allow it to guide you to a time when you flourish, motivate others, and have a long-lasting effect.

VICTOR IMHANS

ABOUT THE AUTHOR

Victor Imhans grasps the complexities of the human mind and helps individuals reach their fullest potential. Unbreakable: Mastering Your Mind, Body, and Life explores the principles and opportunities of mental resilience, physical health, and overall well-being.

Imhans draws on his extensive studies and personal experiences to provide readers with actionable strategies for overcoming mental barriers, enhancing physical well-being, and leading a more balanced and fulfilling life. This writing is both insightful and accessible, making complex psychological concepts easy to understand and apply.

This book, Unbreakable - Mastering Your Mind, Body, and Life, delves into the principles of mental resilience, physical health, and overall life mastery.

www.ingramcontent.com/pod-product-compliance
Lightning Source LLC
Chambersburg PA
CBHW032033040426
42449CB00007B/883